ANTI-INFLAMMATORY DIET

COOKBOOK

*365 DAYS OF EASY RECIPES TO REDUCE
INFLAMMATION & LIVE HEALTHY*

BY DEBBY HAYES

TABLE OF CONTENTS

INTRODUCTION............................5

Inflammation 7

Causes of chronic inflammation 8

Diseases related to chronic inflammation 9

The anti-inflammatory diet:

Eating to prevent and control inflammation. 10

21 DAY MEAL PLAN........................16

BREAKFASTS 17

Quick & Crunchy Strawberry Oats 18

Fruity Coconut Breakfast Squares 19

Coriander & Bean Breakfast Bowls 20

Eggy Vegetable Breakfast Muffins 21

Fruity Arugula & Green Tea Smoothie 22

Savory Yam Breakfast Waffles 23

Blueberry Spiced Granola 24

Very-Berry Banana Pancakes 25

Mini Baked Vegetable Omelets 26

Roasted Yams & Turkey Patties 27

Frozen Yogurt Breakfast Granola 28

Curried Tofu & Veg Scramble 29

Maple-Iced Crumbly Coffee Doughnuts 30

Pumpkin-Spiced Breakfast Waffles 31

Simple Smoked Salmon & Avocado 32

Parsnip & Sausage Breakfast Bake 33

Cauliflower Quiche with Hash Brown Crust 34

SALADS 35

Arugula & Citrus Lentil Salad 36

Quick & Tangy Everything Bagel Salad 37

Crunchy Coriander & Corn Salad 38

Beautiful Berry & Bacon Salad 39

Hearty Greek Beef Salad 40

French Salmon Salad .41

Coriander Shrimp Salad 42

Hearty Bean & Quinoa Salad. 43

Tangy French-Dressed Steak Salad 44

Scrumptious Tuna Salad with Ginger 45

FISH & SEAFOOD..........................46

Ginger Salmon & Bok Choy 47

Fresh Sea Bass & Cauliflower Rice 48

Curried Halibut & Brown Rice 49

Lobster & Angel Hair Pasta. 50

Simple Pesto Halibut & Sprouts 51

Almond-Spiced Mackerel & Veg 52

Zesty Shrimp Skewer Bowls 53

Garlic-Seared Scallops & Spinach 54

Saucy Garlic Mussels .55

Oven-Baked Crab, Mushrooms, & Asparagus . . .56

Honey-Soy Salmon & Veg 57

Simple Shrimp Egg Roll Bowl 58

Stir-Fried Flounder. 59

Deconstructed Sushi Tuna Rolls 60

Coriander-Buttered Cod Fillets 61

Seafood & Coriander Slaw Tacos 62

Shrimp-Stuffed Spaghetti Squash 63

POULTRY 64

Pine Nut Gremolata-Topped Chicken 65

Simple Chicken Shirataki Rice 66

Spinach-Sauced Turkey Meatballs 67

Crispy Chicken & Slaw. 68

Coriander & Avo Chicken Tacos 69

Chicken Parm & Squash Bake 70

Crispy Duck & Yam Mash 72

Citrus-Broiled Ginger Chicken 73

Pork-Crisped Chicken Fingers 74

Cheesy Chicken & Cauliflower Rice 75

BBQ Chicken-Stuffed Zucchini. 76

Ginger-Fried Chicken Quinoa 77

Coriander-Topped Turkey Chili 78
Chicken Mayo-Stuffed Yams 79
Sausage-Stuffed Acorn Squash 80
Zesty Orange & Ginger Chicken 81
Cranberry-Glazed Turkey Fillets 82

BEEF, LAMB, & PORK 83

Pulled Pork & Coriander Wraps 84
Beef Barbacoa Bowls 85
Honey-Roasted Carrots & Chops 86
Beefy Shepherd's Pie & Veg 87
Heart Smart Lamb Wraps 89
Beef & Baked Garlic Mushrooms 90
Honeyed Mongolian Pressure Cooker Beef 91
Shirataki Rice & Pork Balls 92
Sweet & Savory Pineapple Pork 93

VEGETARIAN MAINS 94

Veg & Tempeh Kebabs 95
Mango & Bean Lettuce Wraps 96
Thai-Style Zucchini Noodles 97
Sprouts & Chickpea Salad 98
Garlic Tofu & Avocado Wraps 99
Tahini-Dressed Lentil Salad 100
Nutty Stir-Fried Bok Choy 101
Sweet & Tangy Apple Quinoa 102
Cheesy Vegetarian Pizza 103
Swiss Chard & Strawberry Salad 105
Baked Sprouts in Aioli Sauce 106
Swiss Chard & Bean Quesadillas 107
Fresh Mint Artichoke Risotto 108
Yam & Bean Enchiladas 109
Curried Cauliflower Florets 110
Sweet Smoked Paprika Bean Burgers 111
Avo-Topped Veggie Wraps 112

SOUPS & STEWS 113

Moroccan Spiced Lentil Stew 114
Mexican Spiced Chicken Soup 115
Bell Pepper Rice Soup 116
Turtle Bean & Coriander Soup 117
Asian-Style Noodle Soup 118
Thai-Spiced Chicken Soup 119
Delicious Chard & Tomato Soup 120
Roasted Winter Squash Soup 121
Caramelized Onion Soup 122
Thai-Inspired Shrimp Soup 123
Simple Onion & Mushroom Soup 124
Hearty Curried Chickpea Stew 125
Italian Spinach Soup 126
Vietnamese Beef Soup 127
Beefy Vegetable Stew 128
Gingery Carrot & Turmeric Soup 129

SNACKS & SIDES 130

Lemon Grilled Oysters 131
Coriander & Lime Turtle Beans 132
Greek-Style Flatbread 133
Chocolatey Peanut Butter Bites 134
Coriander & Lime Avocado Hummus 135
Oven-Baked Spinach Chips 136
Ham-Wrapped Cantaloupe Slices 137
Honey-Dipped Rosemary Pecans 138

DESSERTS 139

Nutty Dark Chocolate Bites 140
Pumpkin Spiced Sheet Cheese Cake 141
Chocolate & Honey Chia Pudding 142
Strawberry Maple Pops 143
Coconut Honey Cookies 144
Nutty Honey Brownies 145
Banana Maple Soft Serve 146
Buttery Honey-Dipped Fruit 147

INTRODUCTION

What do diabetes, rheumatoid arthritis, Alzheimer's disease, and cancer have in common? The answer may not be obvious. Diabetes means that your blood sugar levels are poorly controlled. Rheumatoid arthritis means you have stiff, sore joints. Alzheimer's disease means your brain is not working as well as it used to. And cancer means you have a tumor that is making you very sick.

These conditions, and more, may be seemingly unrelated, but underlying each one is chronic inflammation - a state that has only been linked to the development of chronic diseases very recently. Is it the answer medical scientists have been looking for? Could inflammation be the missing link in the management of these diseases?

It is not a big leap to make to imagine that diet and lifestyle interventions that target chronic inflammation offer significant benefits to our health. After all, diets such as the Mediterranean diet and the DASH diet, that have been used for decades, have been shown to help people with weight loss, diabetes, and heart disease, as well as neurological conditions and rheumatoid arthritis.

It is well recognized that a diet that promotes the intake of plenty of plant-based foods, particularly fruits and vegetables, and healthy fats, offers the potential for reducing the risk of developing chronic health conditions. Dietary patterns that minimize the consumption of sugars, refined carbohydrates, and saturated fats prevent inflammation caused by dietary factors. The result is improved physical and mental health.

My dietetics practice is filled with people battling with inflammatory conditions, ranging from obesity to diabetes to arthritis, and heart disease. I find myself saying, "We are dealing with an inflammatory condition here" to about 90% of my patients during their first consultation with me. Most of them nod, and then as the information is processed, the questions start coming. They start to look worried. What exactly do I mean when I refer to chronic inflammation?

Everyone is familiar with the obvious inflammation of a sprained ankle, or the red, angry skin after being struck with an elastic band. It is something we can see, and the cause is pretty clear-cut. So I explain that the inflammation I am referring to, in relation to their health complaint, is hidden within the body. It cannot be seen, and until you present with obesity, diabetes, heart disease, or any other number of conditions, you are unaware that it is a problem.

There are tell-tale signs, though, that inflammation may be on the rise. I can tell that I haven't been eating well when my joints start to feel stiff, or everything starts feeling like it takes more effort than it should. If you are in tune with your body, you can take steps to halt the inflammation in its tracks, and prevent it from developing into a bigger, possibly life-threatening, problem.

The good news is that the changes you have to make are relatively simple. Adding a rainbow of color to your diet, in the form of fruits and vegetables in every shade, may take some effort to begin with. But your body will love you so much for it that before you know it, you won't want to go without.

Healthy, inflammation-preventing, omega-3-rich fats add delicious flavor to your meals and snacks, all while giving your health a boost. No more avoiding fat because you think it makes you fat!

The anti-inflammatory diet is not just about improving your health. I don't believe that is the best reason to make dietary changes. Food is not just about nutrition. It is so much more. We eat for enjoyment. We eat to be sociable and connect with people. We eat because food tastes good. Food is life, and life should be interesting and enjoyable. And that is what the anti-inflammatory diet brings to the table.

The anti-inflammatory diet is a style of eating that should be enjoyed by everyone. Some people are more genetically predisposed to inflammation, but the inflammatory response is something that occurs naturally in every single person. It cannot be avoided altogether, but an unnecessary, chronic inflammatory response can be prevented by making some simple, tasty changes to the food you eat.

INFLAMMATION

What is inflammation?

Inflammation occurs when your body's immune system responds to the damage caused to cells, by bacteria, viruses, or other foreign particles. The cells that have been damaged by these substances release chemicals, such as histamines, in order to trap the offending organisms, and neutralize them so that they cannot cause any more damage to the surrounding cells and tissues. The result can be pain, swelling, bruising, or redness.

If inflammation is contradictory to health, why does the body have an inflammatory response at all?

The inflammatory response is an important part of your immune system. It is the body's first line of defense against disease and damage caused by bacteria, viruses, and toxic substances. Short-lived or acute inflammation is essential to keep us from succumbing to infectious diseases, and preventing wounds from becoming infected. It sends out a signal to the immune system that cells and tissues are damaged, and need to be repaired.

Too much inflammation

When there is too much inflammation over a long period of time, things start going wrong. This is called chronic inflammation. Prolonged inflammation has long-term health implications, and affects the whole body.

It is the result of a small but consistent rise in immune system molecules throughout the body. Chronic inflammation may be the result of a perceived threat to the body. Your body is not necessarily responding to bacteria, viruses, or allergens. It is over reacting to substances that are ordinarily harmless.

The white blood cells that are released to fight the supposed infection, and heal the supposedly damaged cells, have nothing to do. So they find something to do, and it is not good or useful. They start to attack perfectly healthy cells and tissues, which become damaged, and can no longer perform their functions properly.

Eventually, over a long period of time, you start to show the signs of chronic health and/or autoimmune conditions.

CAUSES OF CHRONIC INFLAMMATION

While the basic inflammatory response is the same for everyone, the way your body reacts to invading bacteria and viruses varies. The reasons for this include:

Several risk factors promote a low-level inflammatory response. These include:

- **Age:** Chronic inflammation becomes more common as we get older. It is thought that the energy powerhouses in our cells, the mitochondria, may start to malfunction over time, resulting in an increase in inflammatory molecules in the body. There may also be an accumulation of free-radicals, which cause damage to cells as we age. We also cannot ignore that people tend to accumulate more fat around the abdomen as they move through middle age, and into old age.

- **Obesity:** Fat is not an inactive tissue. It is the largest endocrine organ in the body, secreting many substances, including inflammatory mediators. The higher your body mass, the more inflammatory markers are present in your blood.

- **Diet:** Saturated fats, trans fats, and refined sugars have all been linked to developing chronic inflammation.

- **Smoking:** Exposure to cigarette smoke has been shown to result in the production of fewer anti-inflammatory molecules. It also promotes inflammation.

- **Low Sex Hormones:** Studies have shown that testosterone and estrogen can suppress the production and secretion of several inflammatory substances. Maintaining optimal sex hormone levels helps to reduce the risk of chronic inflammation, and the diseases that are associated with it.

- **Stress:** Physical and emotional stress have been shown to be associated with the release of inflammatory chemicals. Chronic stress can therefore cause chronic inflammation.

- **Sleep Disorders:** Your inability to get a good night's sleep may be related to stress, but if you have a sleeping disorder that is not caused by high levels of stress, you may still be at risk of increased inflammation in your body. A lack of good quality sleep is considered to be an independent risk factor for chronic inflammation.

DISEASES RELATED TO CHRONIC INFLAMMATION

No matter the cause, chronic inflammation has some negative consequences for our health. You may have chronic inflammation if you notice any of the following signs:

- Body pain
- Stiff joints
- Muscle aches
- Chronic fatigue and insomnia
- Depression and anxiety
- Constipation
- Diarrhea
- IBS
- Acid reflux
- Weight changes
- Frequent infections

These are your warning signs. Don't be tempted to pass them off as signs that you are getting old. Your body is letting you know that there is something wrong. Left unchecked, your chronic inflammation may result in any one or more of these health conditions:

- Diabetes
- Cardiovascular disease
- Arthritis and joint diseases
- Allergies
- Asthma
- Chronic obstructive pulmonary disease (COPD)
- Cognitive decline
- Cancer
- Obesity
-

THE ANTI-INFLAMMATORY DIET: EATING TO PREVENT AND CONTROL INFLAMMATION

Is the food you eat your medicine or your poison? Is it making you sick by promoting inflammation in your body, or are you eating food that helps you maintain a healthy immune system?

You cannot control everything that may result in chronic inflammation. Your genes cannot be altered, for example. But you can control how you live, and what you put into your body. If you heed the warning signs, you can take action before chronic inflammation tips over into a more serious health condition.

The best place to start is by addressing your diet, and what you choose to eat. Are you nourishing your body with nutrient-rich foods, or are you causing inflammation by eating calorie-rich, nutrient-poor foods?

There are foods in each food group that will help you stay healthy, and boost your immune system. There are also foods in each food group that will make you ill, and promote inflammation. The problem is, it is something that builds up over time. Unlike the immediate swelling you see after being stung by a bee, chronic inflammation develops over time.

Fats

We have known for a long time that there is a link between a high fat diet, especially one high in saturated fats and trans fats, and chronic disease. What wasn't initially clear to researchers is that high fat diets cause inflammation, and that inflammation underlies almost all chronic diseases. For decades, we were told to follow a low fat diet. Sadly, that has not caused the reduction in the incidence of conditions, such as diabetes and heart disease, that we might have expected.

Medical research continues to delve deeper into what fats do in the body, why they are needed, and which types of fats offer the most benefit to our health. Not all fats are created equal. Some support health, and should be included in your daily diet. Others promote inflammation and disease, and should be limited.

Fats are classified according to their chemical structure:

- **Saturated fats**
- **Unsaturated fats**
  - **Monounsaturated fats**
  - **Polyunsaturated fats**
    - **Omega-3**
    - **Omega-6 fatty acids.**

Some of the fat we consume has been altered during food processing. This is called trans-fat, and behaves similarly to saturated fat in the body.

Inflammatory dietary fats

Trans fats and saturated fats are pro-inflammatory. When your diet contains a lot of these fats, you are more likely to have chronic inflammation, putting yourself at greater risk of developing a chronic disease. Foods to look out for:

Saturated fats	Trans fats
- Fat on meat	- Fried food
- Skin on chicken	- Shortening
- Full fat milk	- Hard brick margarine
- Full fat yoghurt	- Commercially baked cakes
- Cheese	- Cake mixes
- Cream	- Pies
- Butter	- Pie crust
- Coconut oil	- Doughnuts
	- Microwave popcorn
	- Non-dairy coffee creamer

If there is an imbalance in the ratio of omega-6 to omega-3 in the diet, the result is also inflammation. While omega-3 fatty acids help to keep inflammation under control, omega-6 fatty acids are pro-inflammatory. The typical Western diet is full of omega-6 fats. It is estimated that the ratio of omega-6 to omega-3 fats in the Western diet is as high as 20:1. The ideal ratio is between 1:1 and 4:1.

Most fat-containing foods provide a range of different fatty acids in varying quantities. Foods that are high in omega-6 fatty acids include:

Foods high in Omega-6 Fatty Acids
- Sunflower oil
- Corn oil
- Soybean oil
- Grapeseed oil
- Sunflower seeds
- Cottonseed oil

Anti-inflammatory fats:

Omega-3 fatty acids help to fight inflammation in the body. They are considered to be an essential nutrient, because the human body cannot make them; they have to be provided by your diet. Three of the most common omega-3 fatty acids are eicosapentaenoic acid (EPA), docosahexaenoic acid (DHA), and alpha-linoleic acid (ALA). They have all been shown to be beneficial to health, due to their anti-inflammatory properties.

Foods high in omega-3 fatty acids include:

Foods rich in Omega-3 Fatty Acids
- Salmon
- Sardines
- Mackerel
- Anchovies
- Chia seeds
- Walnuts
- Flaxseeds
- Flaxseed oil
- Canola oil

Carbohydrates and sugars

Like fats, there are carbohydrate foods that provide the body with anti-inflammatory nutrients, and those that promote inflammation. It all depends on how much fiber they contain, and how quickly the starches are digested, and released into the blood as glucose.

Sugar has been implicated in chronic inflammation. When your blood sugar levels are constantly raised above the normal 4 to 7 mmol/l, the liver starts to produce free fatty acids. It is these chemicals that stimulate the inflammatory response. Therefore, dietary changes that help to maintain a normal blood sugar level are useful for combating chronic inflammation.

Fiber:

There are two types of fiber in the food we eat:

- **Water soluble fiber** forms a gel in the intestine, which slows down the release of sugar into the blood. It keeps you feeling fuller for longer, and it helps to control your blood sugar levels.

- **Insoluble fiber (roughage)** provides bulk and structure to your stool. It helps to keep your tummy working. Like soluble fiber, it fills you up, and keeps you satisfied until your next meal.

Both types of fiber help to control inflammation in the body in various ways. Because they make you feel full when you eat a fiber-rich meal, they make it easier to control your calorie intake. Therefore, fiber is useful for losing and maintaining your weight. Being overweight is both caused by inflammation, and promotes inflammation. Managing your weight is an important way to reduce chronic inflammation in your body.

Fiber slows down the release of sugar into your blood, making it easier to maintain a normal blood glucose level.

Fiber is a source of fuel for the friendly bacteria living in your gut. Maintaining a balance between friendly bacteria and harmful bacteria in your colon is an essential factor in managing inflammation. When you don't eat enough fiber, the good bacteria that produce anti-inflammatory chemicals die off, and those that trigger an inflammatory response flourish.

Sugars and refined carbohydrates:

The sugar you add to your tea and coffee, the sugar-laden cold drink you enjoy at dinner time, and the biscuits, cakes, chocolates, and sweets you indulge in between meals, all add to your inflammation risk. When you follow an anti-inflammatory diet, it is recommended that you keep these types of foods to an absolute minimum.

Carbohydrate foods to enjoy	Carbohydrate foods to limit
- Whole grain bread	- Sodas
- Brown rice	- Sweets
- Whole wheat pasta	- Chocolates
- Quinoa	- Biscuits
- Oats	- Cakes
- Popcorn	- Pastries
- Sweet potatoes	- White bread
- Beans	- Pasta made from refined flour
- Lentils	
- Chickpeas	

Protein

Whether you eat meat or not, protein is an essential component in the diet. It provides amino acids, which are the building blocks of all proteins, including muscle and other structures, hormones, and enzymes in the body.

Your source of protein is an important consideration when you are eating an anti-inflammatory diet. If you enjoy a good steak, do your research to find out how your meat was raised. Animals that are allowed to graze on grass create fat that has a much better fatty acid profile than those that are grain-fed. Grass-fed beef has a higher concentration of anti-inflammatory omega-3 fatty acids. Grain-fed cattle produce fat that has a higher level of pro-inflammatory omega-6.

Dark, oily fish is the best source of omega-3 fats. It is recommended that you include fish in your diet at least twice a week, to boost your intake of this essential fatty acid.

Plant-based sources of protein - beans, lentils, chickpeas, nuts, soya products - all contain a significant amount of soluble and insoluble fiber, making them a great addition to your weekly meal plan.

Protein foods to include regularly	Protein foods to limit
- Grass-fed beef	- Fried chicken, fish and meat
- Lean red meat	- Chicken with skin
- Skinless chicken	- Grain-fed beef
- Turkey	- Fatty cuts of red meat, such as lamb and mutton
- Dark oily fish	- Hotdogs
- White fish	- Sausages
- Beans	
- Lentils	
- Chickpeas	

Fruits and vegetables

A healthy diet would be incomplete without plenty of fruits and vegetables. They provide most of the vitamins, minerals, and phytonutrients that keep our bodies healthy. They also bring a lot of extra fiber to the table.

Antioxidant vitamins and phytonutrients help to neutralize free radicals that are produced during metabolism, after exposure to toxic chemicals in the environment, and from cigarette smoking. Free radicals are unstable molecules that cause damage to the cells in our bodies. This in turn triggers the inflammatory response to repair the damage.

Vitamins that help to reduce inflammation:

- **Vitamin A**
- **Vitamin B6**
- **Folate**
- **Vitamin B12**
- **Vitamin C**
- **Vitamin D**
- **Vitamin E**
- **Vitamin K**

Phytonutrients have powerful antioxidant and anti-inflammatory properties. They are found in the colors of fruits and vegetables. Including as many different colors in your diet as possible ensures that you are eating a wide variety of these small, but important nutrients. Examples of phytonutrients are:

- **Beta-carotene**
- **Lycopene**
- **Resveratrol**
- **Flavonoids**

Color	Fruits and vegetables
- Orange and yellow	- Carrots - Pumpkin - Turmeric - Orange sweet potatoes - Banana - Mango - Apricots
- Red	- Tomatoes - Radishes - Beetroot - Red cabbage - Red bell peppers - Strawberries - Red apples - Cherries
- Green	- Broccoli - Green beans - Spinach - Cabbage
- Blue and purple	- Purple cabbage - Purple potatoes - Eggplant - Purple cauliflower - Blueberries - Blackberries

Eat a balanced diet to control chronic inflammation

The anti-inflammatory diet is a well-balanced diet, that provides nutrients from all of the food groups. With a focus on bright, colorful fruits and vegetables, omega-3 rich fish, fiber-filled carbohydrates, and only the best quality meat, the exciting ingredients that fill your pantry will translate into scrumptious, inflammation-busting meals.

21 Day Meal Plan

B. Breakfast   *L.* Lunch   *D.* Dinner

DAY 1	DAY 2	DAY 3	DAY 4	DAY 5
B. Quick & Crunchy Strawberry Oats *L.* Ginger Salmon & Bok Choy *D.* Beef & Baked Garlic Mushrooms	*B.* Fruity Coconut Breakfast Squares *L.* Arugula & Citrus Lentil Salad *D.* Cheesy Chicken & Cauliflower Rice	*B.* Coriander & Bean Breakfast Bowls *L.* Spinach Sauced Turkey Meatballs *D.* Hearty Curried Chickpea Stew	*B.* Eggy Vegetable Breakfast Muffins *L.* Quick & Tangy Everything Bagel Salad *D.* Beef & Baked Garlic Mushrooms	*B.* Fruity Arugula & Green Tea Smoothie *L.* Beef Barbacoa Bowls *D.* Coriander-Topped Turkey Chili

DAY 6	DAY 7	DAY 8	DAY 9	DAY 10
B. Savory Yam Breakfast Waffles *L.* Mango & Bean Lettuce Wraps *D.* Fresh Sea Bass & Cauliflower Rice	*B.* Blueberry Spiced Granola *L.* Crunchy Coriander & Corn Salad *D.* Beefy Shepherd's Pie & Veg	*B.* Very-Berry Banana Pancakes *L.* Curried Halibut & Brown Rice *D.* Pine Nut Gremolata Topped Chicken	*B.* Mini-Baked vegetable Omelets *L.* Beautiful Berry & Bacon Salad *D.* Simple Pesto Halibut & Sprouts	*B.* Roasted Yams & Turkey Patties *L.* Thai-Style Zucchini noodles *D.* Shirataki Rice & Pork Balls

DAY 11	DAY 12	DAY 13	DAY 14	DAY 15
B. Frozen Yogurt Breakfast Granola *L.* Hearty Greek Beef Salad *D.* Ginger-Fried Chicken Quinoa	*B.* Curried-Tofu & Veg Scramble *L.* Almond-Spiced Mackerel & Veg *D.* Heart Smart Lamb Wraps	*B.* Maple-Iced Crumbly Coffee Doughnuts *L.* French Salmon Salad *D.* Chicken Mayo Stuffed Yams	*B.* Pumpkin-Spiced Breakfast Waffles *L.* Pulled Pork & Coriander Wraps *D.* Crispy Duck & Yam Mash	*B.* Simple Smoked Salmon & Avocado *L.* Tangy French-Dressed Steak Salad *D.* Curried Halibut & Brown Rice

DAY 16	DAY 17	DAY 18	DAY 19	DAY 20
B. Parsnip & Sausage Breakfast Bake *L.* Simple Shrimp Egg Roll Bowl *D.* Sweet & Savory Pineapple Pork	*B.* Cauliflower Quiche with Hash Brown Crust *L.* Coriander Shrimp Salad *D.* Honey-Roasted Carrots & Chops	*B.* Quick & Crunchy Strawberry Oats *L.* Coriander Slaw & Seafood Tacos *D.* Zesty Orange & Ginger Chicken	*B.* Quick & Crunchy Strawberry Oats *L.* Hearty Bean & Quinoa Salad *D.* Coriander-Buttered Cod Fillets	*B.* Savory Yam Breakfast Waffles *L.* BBQ Chicken-Stuffed Zucchini *D.* Swiss Chard & Bean Quesadillas

DAY 21
B. Blueberry Spiced Granola *L.* Scrumptious Tuna Salad with Ginger *D.* Chicken Parm & Squash Bake

BREAKFASTS

QUICK & CRUNCHY STRAWBERRY OATS

COOK TIME: 0 MINS | MAKES: 2 SERVINGS

INGREDIENTS:

- 1\2 cup raw old-fashioned oats
- 1 cup almond milk
- 1\2 tsp. ground cinnamon
- 2 tsp. raw wild honey
- 1\4 cup store-bought crunchy granola
- 1 cup fresh strawberries, sliced

DIRECTIONS:

1. In an airtight container with a fitted lid, whisk together the raw oats and almond milk. Seal the container, and chill overnight, or for a minimum of 8 hours.

2. When ready to serve, whisk the cinnamon and honey into the chilled oats. Spoon the oats into two separate bowls, and top with granola and strawberries.

3. Serve immediately, and enjoy!

FRUITY COCONUT BREAKFAST SQUARES

COOK TIME: 20 MINS | MAKES: 12 SERVINGS

INGREDIENTS:

- 6 tbsp. pure coconut oil, melted
- 2 tbsp. coconut sugar
- 1\4 cup raw wild honey
- 2 tsp. ground cinnamon
- 1\8 tsp. ground ginger
- 1\8 tsp. ground nutmeg
- 1\2 tsp. baking soda
- 1\2 ripe banana, mashed
- 2 tbsp. collagen peptides powder
- 1\4 cup cassava flour
- 1 cup tiger nut flour
- 2 large free-range eggs
- 1 cup fresh raspberries

DIRECTIONS:

1. Cover a large baking tray with grease-proof paper, and set the oven to preheat to 350°F, with the wire rack in the center of the oven.

2. Place the melted coconut oil, coconut sugar, honey, cinnamon, ginger, and nutmeg in a large bowl. Whisk until all of the ingredients are properly combined. Stir in the baking soda, banana, collagen peptides powder, cassava flour, and tiger nut flour, until properly combined.

3. Beat in the eggs. Gently fold the raspberries into the batter.

4. Use an offset spatula to scrape the batter onto the prepared baking tray. Smooth the batter out in an even layer.

5. Place the tray in the oven for 16-20 minutes, or until the top is golden brown, and the batter is cooked all the way through.

6. Place the tray on the counter for 1-2 hours, or until completely cool. Slice into 12 bars, serve, and enjoy!

Quick Tip:
The bars can be frozen for up to three months, or stored in the cupboard in an airtight container, for no more than 5 days.

CORIANDER & BEAN BREAKFAST BOWLS

COOK TIME: 15 MINS | MAKES: 3 SERVINGS

INGREDIENTS:

- 1 cup savory herbed quinoa
- 3 large free-range eggs
- 1 lime, juiced
- 1\2 tsp. ground cumin
- 15.5 oz. canned black turtle beans, drained and rinsed
- 1 1\2 cups fresh arugula
- Himalayan salt
- Freshly ground black pepper
- 1\4 cup fresh coriander leaves, chopped
- 1 small avocado, sliced

DIRECTIONS:

1. Cook the quinoa according to package instructions, and set aside while you prepare the rest of the dish.

2. Place the eggs in a saucepan, and cover with water. Bring the water to a rolling boil over medium-high heat. Once the water is boiling, transfer the saucepan to a wooden chopping board, and allow the eggs to sit in the water for 11 minutes. Remove the eggs from the water, and set aside to cool.

3. Discard the water from the saucepan before adding in the lime juice, cumin, and black beans. Stir the beans over medium heat for 3-5 minutes, until they are heated through. Transfer the saucepan back to the wooden chopping board, and allow to cool.

4. Divide the fresh arugula between three serving bowls. Top with equal amounts of the cooked quinoa, followed by the beans. Peel the eggs before slicing them in half. Top each bowl with two egg halves. Season to taste with a dash of salt and pepper.

5. Decorate the bowls with fresh coriander leaves and avocado slices. Serve immediately.

Quick Tip:
If preparing ahead of time, store each of the ingredients in separate airtight containers for no more than 5 days. The eggs should remain unpeeled and refrigerated, until you are ready to assemble the bowls.

EGGY VEGETABLE BREAKFAST MUFFINS

COOK TIME: 20 MINS | MAKES: 6 SERVINGS

INGREDIENTS:

- 10 large free-range eggs
- 3\4 tsp. Himalayan salt
- 3\4 tsp. white pepper
- 2 tbsp. fresh chives, chopped
- 2 tbsp. fresh flat-leaf parsley, chopped
- 2 tbsp. fresh basil leaves, finely chopped
- 1 cup broccoli florets, chopped into bite-sized pieces

DIRECTIONS:

1. Thoroughly grease a 12 portion muffin pan with oil, or place 12 silicone cupcake liners in the holders. This is important, as eggs tend to stick while baking, so make sure that you use the liners, or oil the pan thoroughly. Normal baking spray may not prevent the muffins from sticking. Set the oven to preheat to 350°F, with the wire rack in the center of the oven.

2. Crack the eggs into a large bowl, and beat, along with the salt and pepper, until the eggs are frothy. Whisk in the chives, parsley, and chopped basil leaves.

3. Divide the chopped broccoli between the prepared muffin cups, about 1 tablespoon of broccoli per holder.

4. Carefully spoon the egg mixture over the broccoli in the pan, leaving about half an inch at the top.

5. Place the pan in the oven for about 20 minutes, or until the egg is completely set, and the tops are lightly browned.

6. Place the pan on the counter to cool before scooping the muffins onto a serving platter. You may need to use a rubber spatula to loosen the muffins from the pan. Serve immediately.

Quick tip:
The muffins can be stored in the fridge in an airtight container for no more than 5 days, or frozen for no more than 2 months. If freezing, freeze the muffins separately on a baking tray, before freezing them together in an airtight container. This step will prevent the muffins from sticking together while freezing.

FRUITY ARUGULA & GREEN TEA SMOOTHIE

COOK TIME: 2-3 MINS | MAKES: 1 SERVING

INGREDIENTS:

- 1 green tea bag
- 1 cup almond milk
- 3 ice cubes
- 1 tbsp. chia seeds
- 1 cup frozen arugula
- 1\4 cup frozen blueberries
- 1\2 sliced banana, frozen
- 1\2 tsp. ground cinnamon
- 1\4 tsp. nutmeg

DIRECTIONS:

1. Microwave the almond milk on high in a large mug or microwave-safe bowl, stirring at regular intervals to prevent the milk from boiling over. When the milk is boiling hot, add the tea bag, and steep to reach the desired strength.

2. Once the tea is partially cooled, place the ice cubes in the tea.

3. Meanwhile, add the chia seeds, arugula, blueberries, banana, cinnamon, and nutmeg to a high-speed food processor.

4. Pour the lukewarm tea over the ingredients in the food processor, and process on high for 1 minute, until you have a smooth liquid.

5. Serve, and enjoy.

SAVORY YAM BREAKFAST WAFFLES

COOK TIME: 10-15 MINS | MAKES: 2 SERVINGS

INGREDIENTS:

Waffles:
- 1\8 tsp. sweet smoked paprika
- 1\4 tsp. Himalayan salt
- 1\2 tsp. garlic powder
- 1 large yam, scrubbed and finely grated
- 2 large free-range eggs

Filling:
- 4 oz. nitrate-free, sugar-free bacon strips (4 strips)

- 3 cups fresh spinach, stemmed and chopped
- 1\4 tsp. Himalayan salt
- 1\8 tsp. white pepper
- 2 large free-range eggs
- 1\2 avocado, peeled, pitted, sliced

Sriracha aioli:
- 2 tsp. sriracha
- 1\4 cup paleo mayonnaise

DIRECTIONS:

1. Preheat a waffle iron while you mix the batter. When the iron is hot, lightly coat the surface with baking spray.

2. In a large bowl, whisk together the sweet smoked paprika, salt, garlic powder, grated yam, and eggs. Scoop the batter into the prepared waffle iron, using an offset spatula to spread it out in an even layer. Close the waffle iron, and cook the waffles for 5-7 minutes, or until golden brown and properly cooked.

3. Meanwhile, heat a large, non-stick frying pan over medium-high heat before adding the bacon strips. Fry the bacon for 2-3 minutes, until the edges are nice and crispy. Transfer the cooked bacon to a paper-towel-lined plate.

4. Discard all but 3 tablespoons of the bacon fat from the pan. Add the spinach to the pan, along with the salt and pepper. Toss for 2-3 minutes, until the leaves wilt. Make a well in the center of the spinach, and crack in the eggs, taking care not to damage the yolks. Fry the eggs for 2 minutes, or until the whites are no longer runny. Carefully flip the eggs, and fry for 1 additional minute before transferring the pan to a wooden chopping board.

5. In a small glass bowl, whisk together the sriracha and mayonnaise.

6. Divide the waffles between two plates. On each plate, top one waffle with two strips of bacon, half of the cooked spinach, and one fried egg. Garnish with half the avocado, and drizzle with aioli. Close the sandwiches with the remaining waffles. Serve hot.

BLUEBERRY SPICED GRANOLA

COOK TIME: 20-40 MINS | MAKES: 6 SERVINGS

INGREDIENTS:

- 1-inch fresh ginger, finely grated
- 1\3 tsp. ground cinnamon
- 1\3 tsp. ground nutmeg
- 1\4 tsp. kosher salt
- 2 tbsp. chia seeds
- 1 cup lightly toasted almond slivers

- 3 cups old-fashioned rolled oats
- 1 tsp. pure vanilla essence
- 1\3 cup sunflower oil
- 1\2 cup pure maple syrup
- 2 cups fresh blueberries
- Plain Greek yogurt or soy milk for serving (optional)

DIRECTIONS:

1. Cover a large baking tray with grease-proof paper, and set the oven to preheat to 325°F, with the wire rack in the center of the oven.

2. Place the ginger, cinnamon, nutmeg, salt, chia seeds, almond slivers, and rolled oats in a large mixing bowl. Stir with a wooden spoon to combine.

3. In a separate medium-sized bowl, whisk together the vanilla, sunflower oil, and syrup.

4. Scrape the syrup mixture into the bowl of oats and spices, stirring to combine.

5. Gently fold in the fresh blueberries until evenly distributed.

6. Scrape the mixture onto your prepared baking sheet, and use the wooden spoon to spread it out as evenly as possible.

7. Place the tray in the oven for 20 minutes, then stir and flip the granola. Return the tray to the oven for an additional 20 minutes. The edges of the granola should be lightly browned. Keep an eye on the granola, as it tends to burn quickly.

8. Let cool completely before serving or storing.

9. Serve the granola with optional yogurt or soy milk.

Quick Tip:
The granola can be refrigerated for up to 5 days in an airtight container, or frozen for no more than 2 months. Freeze the granola in separate portions to make thawing easier for single use.

VERY-BERRY BANANA PANCAKES

COOK TIME: 5-10 MINS | MAKES: 2 SERVINGS

INGREDIENTS:

- 1 medium orange, juiced
- 1 cup cherries, pitted
- 1 cup strawberries, hulled and sliced
- 1 cup blueberries
- 1\4 tsp. baking soda
- 2 large free-range eggs, beaten
- 2 ripe bananas, mashed
- 1 tbsp. coconut oil

DIRECTIONS:

1. In a small pot over medium-high heat, whisk together the orange juice, and all three cups of berries. When the juice begins to boil, lower the heat to medium-low, and simmer the fruit for 10-12 minutes. Stir at regular intervals, and partially break some of the fruit as you go. When the juice begins to thicken, transfer the pot to a wooden chopping board, and allow to cool. The sauce will become thicker as the mixture cools.

2. Meanwhile, whisk together the baking soda, eggs, and mashed bananas in a medium-sized bowl.

3. Heat the coconut oil in a large frying pan over medium-high heat. When the oil is nice and hot, pour 1\4 cup of the batter into the pan. Fry the pancake for 4-5 minutes, or until the middle is set, and the edges are browned. Flip the pancake, and fry for an additional 1-2 minutes. Remove the pancake onto a plate, and keep warm while you repeat the process with the remaining batter.

4. Divide the pancakes between two plates, and top with the cooled berry sauce before serving.

Quick Tip:
The pancakes can be refrigerated in an airtight container for no more than 2 days. Store the berry sauce in the fridge in a sealed glass jar for no more than 5 days. Reheat the pancakes and sauce in the microwave for 2-3 minutes before serving.

MINI BAKED VEGETABLE OMELETS

COOK TIME: 10 MINS | MAKES: 6 SERVINGS

INGREDIENTS:

- 1 cup broccoli florets, finely chopped
- 2 tbsp. water
- 1\2 tsp. Himalayan salt
- 1\2 tsp. white pepper
- 1\4 cup fresh flat-leaf parsley, chopped
- 1\4 cup spring onions, chopped
- 1\2 cup frozen Swiss chard, thawed, and squeezed dry
- 8 large free-range eggs, yolks and whites separated

DIRECTIONS:

1. Lightly spray a 24-cup muffin pan with baking spray, and set the oven to preheat to 350°F, with the wire rack in the center of the oven.

2. Place the broccoli florets in a large glass bowl, and toss to coat with 2 tablespoons of water. Seal the bowl with cling wrap, and microwave on high until soft, about 2 minutes. Remove the cling wrap, and let cool on the counter.

3. When the broccoli is nicely cooled, add the salt, pepper, parsley, spring onions, chard, and egg yolks, stirring with a wooden spoon to combine.

4. Place the egg whites in a large mixing bowl, and beat on high for 2 minutes with an electric hand mixer, until the whites form stiff peaks. Gently fold 1\3 of the egg whites into the bowl of broccoli. Repeat the process until all of the beaten egg whites are properly incorporated.

5. Divide the mixture between the 24 cups in the muffin pan, and bake in the oven for 8 minutes, or until the eggs are set, and the edges are golden brown.

6. Remove the pan from the oven, and allow the mini omelets to cool in the pan for 2 minutes before carefully transferring them to a cooling rack. Serve slightly cooled, or cold.

Quick Tip:
The mini omelets can be refrigerated for no more than 5 days in an airtight container.

ROASTED YAMS & TURKEY PATTIES

COOK TIME: 25-30 MINS | MAKES: 4 SERVINGS

INGREDIENTS:

- 2 large yams, scrubbed and cubed (1\2-inch cubes)
- 2 tbsp. extra-virgin avocado oil
- 1\2 tsp. freshly ground black pepper (divided)
- 1 tsp. Himalayan salt (divided)
- 1\2 tsp. onion powder
- 1 tsp. paprika
- 1 1\2 tsp. garlic powder
- Pinch of ground nutmeg (optional)
- 1\2 tsp. crushed fennel seeds
- 1 1\2 tsp. fresh rosemary, chopped
- 1 tbsp. fresh sage, chopped
- 2 tbsp. pure maple syrup
- 1 lb. ground turkey

DIRECTIONS:

1. Line a large, rimmed baking tray with tin foil, and set the oven to preheat to 400°F, with the wire rack in the center of the oven.

2. In a large mixing bowl, toss together the yam cubes, avocado oil, half of the black pepper, half of the salt, onion powder, paprika, and garlic powder, until the yam cubes are evenly coated in the spices and oil. Fan the coated cubes out on the prepared baking pan in an even layer. Roast the cubes in the oven for 15 minutes.

3. Meanwhile, in the same bowl you used to toss the yams, add together the remaining salt and pepper, along with the nutmeg, fennel seeds, rosemary, sage, maple syrup, and turkey. Use a wooden spoon to stir the ingredients together until properly combined.

4. When the yams have been in the oven for 15 minutes, transfer the pan to a wooden chopping board. Flip the yams using a spatula, and push them all to one side of the pan, making room for the patties.

5. Using your hands, form the turkey mixture into 12 patties of roughly the same size. Space the patties about 1-inch apart on the pan, next to the roasted yams.

6. Place the pan back in the oven for 1o minutes. After 10 minutes, flip the patties and yams once again, before turning the oven up to broil. Broil for 2-3 minutes, or until the patties are cooked all the way through, and the yams are crispy around the edges.

7. Remove the pan from the oven, and serve immediately.

FROZEN YOGURT BREAKFAST GRANOLA

COOK TIME: 0 MINS | MAKES: 4 SERVINGS

INGREDIENTS:

- 1\2 cup fresh blueberries
- 1 tbsp. fresh lemon juice
- 2 tbsp. raw wild honey
- 7 oz. plain, low-fat Greek yogurt
- 1\3 cup shredded coconut
- 1 tsp. pure vanilla extract
- 2\3 cup gluten-free, whole-grain, store-bought granola

DIRECTIONS:

1. In a large mixing bowl, stir together the blueberries, lemon juice, honey, yogurt, coconut, and vanilla extract. Use the spoon to smash the blueberries against the side of the bowl as you go, leaving about half intact.

2. Scrape the yogurt mixture onto a large, rimmed baking pan covered in tinfoil or grease-proof paper. Spread the mixture out in an even layer of about 1 1\4-inches thick.

3. Drizzle the granola over the yogurt mixture, breaking up any large clumps. Use clean hands to gently press the granola down into the yogurt.

4. Place the pan in the freezer for at least an hour. When the yogurt is properly frozen, break the contents of the pan into bite-sized portions, and serve immediately.

Quick Tip:
Any leftover granola should be returned to the freezer immediately. This recipe should be eaten quickly once served, to prevent melting.

CURRIED TOFU & VEG SCRAMBLE

COOK TIME: 10 MINS | MAKES: 2 SERVINGS

INGREDIENTS:

- 1 tbsp. extra-virgin olive oil
- 1 cup asparagus, chopped
- 1 garlic clove, minced
- 1\2 small shallot, diced
- 1 cup Swiss chard, chopped
- 8 oz. firm tofu, pressed with paper towels, and crumbled
- 1\2 tsp. Himalayan salt
- 1\2 tsp. ground turmeric powder
- 1\2 tsp. freshly ground black pepper

DIRECTIONS:

1. Heat the oil in a large frying pan over medium heat. When the oil is nice and hot, fry the asparagus, garlic, and shallots for 3-5 minutes, until the asparagus is fork-tender, and the onions are no longer opaque. Toss in the chard, and continue to cook for a few minutes while stirring, until the leaves have wilted.

2. Crumble the tofu into the pan, and continue to fry for 4-5 minutes, until the edges are golden brown. If the tofu sticks to the pan, add a few splashes of water, and scrape the bottom of the pan to prevent burning. Stir in the salt, turmeric, and black pepper until properly incorporated. Remove the pan from the heat, and allow to cool slightly.

3. Divide the scramble between two plates, and serve warm.

Quick Tip:
The scramble can be refrigerated in an airtight container for no more than 5 days. To reheat, microwave on high for 1-2 minutes.

MAPLE-ICED CRUMBLY COFFEE DOUGHNUTS

COOK TIME: 22-25 MINS | MAKES: 9 SERVINGS

INGREDIENTS:

Crumble:
- 1\4 tsp. kosher salt
- 1\2 tsp. ground cinnamon
- 1\3 tsp. ground nutmeg
- 1\3 cup coconut sugar
- 3 tbsp. tapioca flour
- 3\4 cup almond flour
- 1\3 cup coconut oil at room temperature

Doughnuts:
- 1\4 tsp. kosher salt
- 1\2 tsp. baking soda
- 2 tsp. ground cinnamon

- 1\4 cup tapioca flour
- 2\3 cup coconut flour
- 1 tsp. pure vanilla essence
- 2 tbsp. coconut oil, melted and slightly cooled
- 1\3 cup well-shaken full fat coconut milk
- 1\2 cup pure maple syrup
- 4 large free-range eggs at room temperature

Icing:
- 3 tbsp. pure maple syrup
- 2 tbsp. tapioca flour
- 1\4 cup almond butter, melted
- 2-3 tbsp. water

DIRECTIONS:

1. Lightly coat 9 holes of a 12-hole doughnut mold with baking spray, and set the oven to preheat to 350°F, with the wire rack in the center of the oven.

2. In a large bowl, whisk together the salt, cinnamon, nutmeg, sugar, tapioca flour, and almond flour. Add the coconut oil at room temperature, and use sharp knives to cut the mixture into crumbs to make the crumble. Set aside.

3. To make the doughnuts, place the salt, baking soda, cinnamon, tapioca flour, and coconut flour in a medium-sized bowl, and whisk until all of the ingredients are properly combined.

4. Place the vanilla, coconut oil, coconut milk, maple syrup, and eggs in the large bowl of a stand mixer. Beat the mixture for a few minutes, until light and fluffy. With the mixer running, gradually pour in the flour mixture until just combined. Do not over mix the batter.

5. Divide the mixture between the nine greased doughnut holes. Sprinkle the set aside crumble over the top of each doughnut. Place the mold in the oven for 22-25 minutes, or until an inserted skewer comes out clean, and the tops are lightly toasted. Remove the mold from the oven, and allow the doughnuts to cool in the mold for 15 minutes before transferring to a rack, and cooling completely.

6. While the doughnuts are cooling, in a small glass bowl, whisk together the maple syrup, tapioca flour, and almond butter. Add the water 1 tablespoon at a time, until the icing reaches drizzling consistency.

7. Drizzle the icing over the cooled doughnuts before serving.

PUMPKIN-SPICED BREAKFAST WAFFLES

COOK TIME: 10 MINS | MAKES: 4 SERVINGS

INGREDIENTS:

- 1\2 tsp. ground cinnamon
- 1\8 tsp. ground ginger
- 1\8 tsp. ground nutmeg
- 1 1\2 cups cassava flour
- 1\2 cup tiger nut flour
- 1\2 tsp. flaky sea salt
- 1 tsp. baking powder
- 1\2 tsp. baking soda
- 1\4 cup coconut sugar
- 2 tbsp. beef gelatin powder
- ½ cup pumpkin puree
- ½ cup coconut oil, melted
- 1 tsp. pure vanilla essence
- filtered water, as needed

DIRECTIONS:

1. Preheat a waffle iron coated in baking spray.

2. In a food processor, combine the cinnamon, ginger, nutmeg, cassava flour, tiger nut flour, sea salt, baking powder, baking soda, coconut sugar, beef gelatin powder, pumpkin puree, coconut oil, and vanilla. Process on high for a minute or two, until you have a lump-free batter. If the batter isn't pourable, add filtered water, 1 tablespoon at a time, and process until the batter reaches the desired consistency.

3. If you have a waffle iron that can yield four waffles at a time, divide the batter between the four molds, smooth out the tops, and close the waffle iron. Cook the waffles according to the waffle iron instructions. The waffles should be cooked all the way through, and golden brown. If you do not have an iron that cooks four waffles at a time, you will have to divide the batter, and cook in batches.

4. Serve the waffles hot, with a topping of your choice.

Quick Tip:
Waffles can be refrigerated for up to five days in an airtight container, or frozen for no more than three months.

SIMPLE SMOKED SALMON & AVOCADO

COOK TIME: 0 MINS | MAKES: 2 SERVINGS

INGREDIENTS:

- 8 oz. smoked wild salmon
- 1 Hass avocado, pitted, peeled, and sliced
- 2 tbsp. mayonnaise
- 1 tbsp. capers
- 1 tbsp. fresh dill, chopped
- Freshly ground black pepper
- Himalayan salt

DIRECTIONS:

1. Divide the salmon between two plates, and top with the avocado slices. Place a dollop of mayonnaise on the top, and garnish with the capers and dill. Season to taste with salt and pepper.

2. Serve immediately, and enjoy.

Quick Tip:
Salmon can easily be replaced with tuna or cooked shrimp.

PARSNIP & SAUSAGE BREAKFAST BAKE

COOK TIME: 30 MINS | MAKES: 4 SERVINGS

INGREDIENTS:

- 6 parsnips, peeled, and roughly chopped
- 2 tbsp. extra-virgin olive oil
- 2 garlic cloves, minced
- 1 small shallot, diced
- 1 lb. pork sausages, chopped
- 1\2 tsp. crushed thyme (divided)
- 1 tsp. kosher salt (divided)
- ¼ cup full-fat, unsweetened coconut milk
- 6 slices bacon, cooked, and chopped

DIRECTIONS:

1. Set the oven to preheat to 350°F, with the wire rack in the center of the oven.

2. Place the parsnips in a large pot, and cover with water. Bring the water to a rolling boil over medium heat. Once the water begins to boil, cook the parsnips until softened, about 15 minutes.

3. Meanwhile, in a large, oven-proof frying pan, heat the olive oil. When the oil is nice and hot, fry the garlic and shallots for 5 minutes, or until the shallots become translucent. Add the sausage, half of the thyme, and half of the salt. Cook the sausage for 5-8 minutes, stirring continuously until golden brown.

4. Pour the softened parsnips through a colander, and drain properly before transferring to a high power food processor. Add the remaining salt and thyme, along with the coconut milk. Pulse on high until you have a smooth paste. Scrape the parsnip paste into the pan with the sausages, and stir to combine, smoothing out the surface using an offset spatula.

5. Sprinkle the bacon over the top. Place the pan in the oven for 15 minutes, or until the top is golden brown. Serve immediately.

Quick Tip:
Any leftovers can be refrigerated for 3-4 days in an airtight container.

CAULIFLOWER QUICHE WITH HASH BROWN CRUST

COOK TIME: 60 MINS | MAKES: 8 SERVINGS

INGREDIENTS:

Cauliflower:
- 3 cups small cauliflower florets
- 2 tbsp. extra-virgin avocado oil
- 1\2 tsp. kosher salt
- 1\8 tsp. white pepper
- 1 tsp. garlic powder

Hash brown crust:
- 2 lbs. Yukon gold potatoes, peeled and grated
- 1 tsp. kosher salt
- 1\4 tsp. freshly ground black pepper
- 3 tbsp. extra-virgin avocado oil

Quiche:
- 2 tbsp. fresh flat-leaf parsley, minced
- 2 tbsp. fresh basil leaves, minced
- 1\4 cup fresh tarragon, chopped
- 1 cup unsweetened almond milk
- 8 large free-range eggs
- 1 tsp. kosher salt
- 1\4 tsp. white pepper
- Fresh arugula for topping

DIRECTIONS:

1. Line a large, rimmed baking tray with greaseproof paper, and set the oven to preheat to 350°F, with the wire rack in the center of the oven.

2. In a large bowl, toss the cauliflower with the avocado oil, salt, pepper, and garlic powder, until the florets are evenly coated. Spread the seasoned florets out in an even layer on the prepared baking tray. Bake in the oven for 20 minutes, stirring halfway through the cooking time. The cauliflower should be nicely browned around the edges. Set aside to cool.

3. Place the grated potatoes in the center of a clean kitchen towel, bundle them up, and squeeze as much water from the bundle as possible. Transfer the potatoes to a large mixing bowl, and stir in the salt and pepper.

4. In a large, oven-safe frying pan, heat the oil, tilting the pan to coat the bottom and sides. When the oil is nice and hot, scrape the seasoned potatoes into the pan. Use an off-set spatula to press and mold the potatoes into a crust. Continue to form and press the potatoes into a crust on the heat, for about 10-12 minutes, or until the edges begin to crisp. Transfer the pan to a wooden chopping board.

5. In a large mixing bowl, whisk together the parsley, basil, tarragon, almond milk, eggs, salt, and pepper.

6. Scrape the cauliflower into the potato crust in an even layer. Pour the egg mixture over the cauliflower.

7. Place the pan in the oven for 45-50 minutes, or until the eggs are no longer runny, and the top is nicely browned.

8. Garnish the quiche with fresh arugula, slice, and serve hot.

SALADS

ARUGULA & CITRUS LENTIL SALAD

COOK TIME: 40 MINS | MAKES: 5 SERVINGS

INGREDIENTS:

- 4 cups vegetable stock
- 2 cups green dhal lentils
- Store-bought citrus vinaigrette dressing
- 10 cups fresh arugula
- 1\4 cup fresh dill, chopped

DIRECTIONS:

1. Stir together the stock and lentils in a large pot over high heat. When the stock begins to boil, reduce the heat to medium-low. Simmer the lentils, stirring at regular intervals, until they are tender, and most of the stock has reduced, about 25-30 minutes.

2. Transfer the pot to a wooden chopping board, and stir in the citrus dressing. Set aside to marinate while you prepare the rest of the dish.

3. Divide the arugula between 5 serving bowls, and top with the citrus-coated dhal. Garnish with dill, and serve.

Quick Tip:
Leftover dhal can be refrigerated in an airtight container for no more than 5 days, or frozen for up to 3 months. To thaw, leave the dhal in the fridge overnight, and reheat on the stove for 2-3 minutes before serving with fresh salad greens.

QUICK & TANGY EVERYTHING BAGEL SALAD

COOK TIME: 0 MINS | MAKES: 6 SERVINGS

INGREDIENTS:

- 1 cooked rotisserie chicken
- 1\2 lime, juiced
- 2 tsp. French mustard
- 1 cup paleo mayonnaise
- 2 tbsp. Everything Bagel seasoning
- 1\4 cup red onion, diced
- 1 celery stalk, finely chopped
- 1 cup grapes, sliced in half
- Fresh parsley for garnish

DIRECTIONS:

1. In a large bowl, de-bone and shred all the chicken, discarding the skin and bones.

2. Stir in the lime juice, mustard, mayonnaise, Everything Bagel seasoning, onion, celery, and grapes.

3. Plate the salad, and garnish with parsley before serving. Enjoy the tangy taste!

CRUNCHY CORIANDER & CORN SALAD

COOK TIME: 0 MINS | MAKES: 2 SERVINGS

INGREDIENTS:

- 2 tablespoons roasted unsalted pumpkin seeds
- 1\4 cup fresh Mexican cheese, crumbled
- 2 tbsp. fresh coriander leaves, chopped
- 2\3 cup no-salt-added canned black turtle beans
- 1\2 cup fresh corn kernels
- 1\2 cup cherry tomatoes, halved
- 6 cups romaine lettuce, chopped
- 1\4 tsp. ground cumin
- 1\4 tsp. Himalayan salt
- Freshly ground black pepper to taste
- 1 tsp. raw wild honey
- 2 tbsp. fresh lime juice
- 4 tsp. extra-virgin olive oil

DIRECTIONS:

1. In a large mixing bowl, toss together the pumpkin seeds, Mexican cheese, coriander leaves, black turtle beans, corn kernels, tomatoes, and lettuce.

2. In a small glass bowl, whisk together the cumin, salt, pepper, honey, lime juice, and olive oil.

3. Drizzle the dressing over the salad, and toss to coat. Serve immediately.

BEAUTIFUL BERRY & BACON SALAD

COOK TIME: 10 MINS | MAKES: 1 SERVING

INGREDIENTS:

- 3 strips thick-cut bacon
- 1\2 Hass avocado, pitted, peeled, and diced
- 3 cups fresh arugula, chopped
- 1\2 cup strawberries, trimmed and halved
- 1 tsp. crushed garlic
- 2 tbsp. balsamic vinegar
- Himalayan salt
- Freshly ground black pepper

DIRECTIONS:

1. Fry the bacon for about ten minutes in a large frying pan over medium heat, until the edges are nice and crispy. Carefully place the bacon on a paper-towel-lined plate to cool. When the bacon is cool enough to handle, coarsely chop the strips into small pieces. Scoop the pieces into a salad bowl.

2. Add the avocado, arugula, strawberries, and garlic, and toss to combine. Drizzle with the balsamic vinegar, and season to taste with salt and pepper. Serve immediately.

HEARTY GREEK BEEF SALAD

COOK TIME: 20 MINS | MAKES: 1 SERVING

INGREDIENTS:

- 6 oz. skirt steak
- 1\2 tsp. flaky sea salt
- 2 tbsp. sunflower oil
- 1\2 Hass avocado, pitted, peeled, and sliced
- 1\4 cup thinly sliced red onion
- 1\4 cup English cucumber, diced
- 2 cups mixed salad greens
- 2 tsp. dried oregano
- 1\4 cup extra-virgin olive oil
- 1\2 lime, juiced

DIRECTIONS:

1. Place the steak on a wooden chopping board, and season each side with sea salt. Heat the oil in a large frying pan over high heat, and when the oil is nice and hot, fry the steak for 2-3 minutes per side for rare, 3-4 minutes for medium-rare, or 5-7 minutes for well-done.

2. Return the steak to the chopping board, and cool for 10 minutes before slicing it into strips against the grain.

3. Combine the avocado, onion, cucumber, and salad greens in a large mixing bowl, along with the steak strips.

4. In a small glass bowl, whisk together the oregano, olive oil, and lime juice.

5. Drizzle the dressing over the salad, and toss to coat. Serve immediately.

FRENCH SALMON SALAD

COOK TIME: 10 MINS | MAKES: 2 SERVINGS

INGREDIENTS:

- 2 salmon fillets, patted dry
- Kosher salt
- 1 tbsp. sunflower oil
- 1 tsp. crushed garlic
- 2 tbsp. balsamic vinegar
- 1\4 cup extra-virgin olive oil
- Freshly ground black pepper
- 4 cups mixed salad greens
- 1\4 cup thinly sliced red radish
- 1\4 cup pitted brown olives
- 1\4 cup thinly sliced red onion
- 1\4 cup diced English cucumber

DIRECTIONS:

1. Season the salmon fillets on both sides with a generous pinch of salt.

2. In a large frying pan over medium heat, heat the sunflower oil. When the oil is nice and hot, fry the salmon for 3-4 minutes per side.

3. In a small glass bowl, whisk together the garlic and vinegar. Gradually drizzle in the olive oil while whisking. Taste the dressing, and add a pinch of salt and pepper if desired.

4. Divide the mixed salad greens, radish slices, olives, sliced onion, and cucumber between two serving bowls. Top each salad bowl with a fried salmon fillet.

5. Season the contents of the bowls with the dressing, and serve.

CORIANDER SHRIMP SALAD

COOK TIME: 5 MINS | MAKES: 1 SERVING

INGREDIENTS:

- 6 oz. shrimp, peeled and deveined
- 2 cups mixed salad greens
- 1 spring onion, finely chopped
- 1 avocado, pitted, peeled, and diced
- 1\4 cup store-bought lime vinaigrette
- 1\2 cup chopped coriander leaves
- Himalayan salt
- Freshly ground black pepper

DIRECTIONS:

1. Bring a small pot of water to a rolling boil over high heat. When the water is boiling, add the shrimp, and cook for 2-3 minutes, until the shrimp blush, and the tails curl into a C. Immediately dunk the cooked shrimp in a bowl of ice water to stop the cooking process. Transfer the cooled shrimp to a paper towel-lined plate.

2. In a large bowl, toss together the mixed salad greens, spring onions, avocado, and dried shrimp.

3. In a small glass bowl, whisk together the lime vinaigrette and coriander leaves. Season to taste with salt and pepper.

4. Drizzle the dressing over the salad, and toss to coat. Serve immediately, and enjoy.

Quick Tip:
Frozen shrimp should be thawed under cool water before cooking.

HEARTY BEAN & QUINOA SALAD

COOK TIME: 20 MINS | MAKES: 5 SERVINGS

INGREDIENTS:

- 2 cups water
- 1 cup quinoa, rinsed
- 1 tsp. Himalayan salt
- 1 tsp. white pepper
- 2 tsp. ground cumin
- 2 lemons, juiced
- 2 1\2 tbsp. extra-virgin olive oil
- 1\2 cup diced red onion
- 15.5 oz. canned black turtle beans, drained and rinsed
- 1 1\2 cups fresh corn kernels
- 1 large Hass avocado, thinly sliced
- 1\2 cup fresh coriander leaves, chopped

DIRECTIONS:

1. Whisk the water and quinoa together in a medium-sized pot over high heat. When the water begins to boil, allow to simmer for 15 minutes over medium-low heat with the lid on the pot, stirring occasionally to prevent burning. Transfer the pot to a wooden chopping board when the water has reduced, and the quinoa is tender.

2. In a large mixing bowl, whisk together the salt, pepper, cumin, lemon juice, olive oil, and onion. Add the black beans, corn kernels, and cooked quinoa, stirring to combine.

3. Spoon the mixture into 5 serving bowls, and top with the sliced avocado, and coriander leaves. Serve immediately.

Quick Tip:
Leftover salad can be refrigerated in an airtight container for no more than 5 days.

TANGY FRENCH-DRESSED STEAK SALAD

COOK TIME: 0 MINS | MAKES: 2 SERVINGS

INGREDIENTS:

- 6 oz. cooked lean steak, cooled and chopped
- 1\3 cup thinly sliced red onion
- 3 cups mixed salad greens
- 1 large orange
- 1\4 tsp. Himalayan salt
- Pinch of freshly ground black pepper to taste
- 1\2 tsp. French mustard
- 1 tbsp. balsamic vinegar
- 2 tbsp. extra-virgin olive oil
- 1\2 ripe avocado, chopped

DIRECTIONS:

1. Divide the chopped steak, red onion, and mixed salad greens between 2 serving bowls, and toss to combine.

2. Peel and section the orange over a large mixing bowl. Cut the sections into thirds, catching any juices in the bowl. Liberally scatter the chopped orange sections over the salad bowls.

3. In the bowl with the orange juice, whisk in the salt, pepper, mustard, balsamic vinegar, and olive oil. Drizzle the vinegar mixture over the salads, and add the sliced avocado.

4. Lightly toss the salads, and serve.

SCRUMPTIOUS TUNA SALAD WITH GINGER

COOK TIME: 6 MINS | MAKES: 1 SERVING

INGREDIENTS:

- 2 tsp. fresh ginger, grated
- 2 tsp. crushed garlic
- 2 tsp. lemon juice
- 2 tbsp. extra-virgin olive oil (divided)
- 1\4 cup coconut aminos
- 1 ahi tuna steak
- 1\2 avocado, pitted, peeled, and diced
- 1\2 English cucumber, diced
- 1 cup purple cabbage, shredded
- Himalayan salt
- Freshly ground black pepper

DIRECTIONS:

1. In a medium-sized mixing bowl, whisk together the ginger, garlic, lemon juice, 1 tablespoon of olive oil, and coconut aminos. Divide the marinade between 2 airtight containers. Submerge the steak in one of the containers. Seal both containers, and chill for 10 minutes.

2. After 10 minutes, remove the container with the tuna, and pour off the marinade. Pat the steak dry with paper towels.

3. In a large frying pan over medium heat, heat the remaining olive oil. When the oil is nice and hot, sear the steak for 2-3 minutes per side. You may fry the tuna for a few more minutes if you prefer well-done tuna.

4. In a salad bowl, toss together the avocado, cucumber, and cabbage. Season to taste with salt and pepper before drizzling with the reserved chilled dressing.

5. Place the seared tuna on top of the salad, and serve.

FISH & SEAFOOD

GINGER SALMON & BOK CHOY

COOK TIME: 10 MINS | MAKES: 2 SERVINGS

INGREDIENTS:

- 1 skin-on wild salmon fillet, patted dry
- 1\4 tsp. flaky sea salt
- 2 tbsp. coconut aminos (plus 2 tsp.)
- 2 tsp. fresh ginger, grated (divided)
- 3 tsp. extra-virgin olive oil (divided)
- 3 tsp. crushed garlic
- 1\2 lb. baby bok choy, cut in half lengthwise

DIRECTIONS:

1. Place the salmon fillet on a wooden chopping board, and season both sides with the salt.

2. In a medium-sized mixing bowl, whisk together the coconut aminos and 1 teaspoon of fresh ginger. Coat the seasoned salmon in the mixture, and cover the bowl with cling wrap. Chill for 20 minutes.

3. Heat two teaspoons of olive oil in a large frying pan over medium-high heat. When the oil is nice and hot, add the remaining ginger, and the garlic, and fry for 2 minutes. Stir in the remaining coconut aminos, and the bok choy. Toss the bok choy in the pan for an additional 2 minutes, or until the leaves begin to crisp. Scrape the contents of the pan into a large bowl, and keep warm.

4. Return the pan to the heat, and add the remaining olive oil. Over medium heat, fry the salmon, skin side down for 6 minutes. Reserve the marinade. Keep an eye on the heat to prevent the salmon from burning.

5. After 6 minutes, flip the fish, and add the marinade to the pan. Simmer the fish for an additional 2 minutes, or until it is properly cooked, and opaque.

6. Devide the cooked bok choy between two serving bowls and top with the salmon. Drizzle the juices from the pan over everything in the bowls and serve.

Quick Tip:
Any leftovers can be refrigerated in an airtight container for no more than 5 days.

FRESH SEA BASS & CAULIFLOWER RICE

COOK TIME: 12 MINS | MAKES: 2 SERVINGS

INGREDIENTS:

- 1 tsp. fish sauce
- 2 tbsp. coconut aminos
- 1 tsp. fresh ginger, grated
- 1 tsp. crushed garlic
- 2 sea bass fillets
- 2 tsp. extra-virgin olive oil
- 1 cup fresh, store-bought cauliflower rice
- 1 spring onion, thinly chopped

DIRECTIONS:

1. In a large mixing bowl, whisk together the fish sauce, coconut aminos, ginger, and garlic. Coat the fillets in the marinade, cover, and chill for 2o minutes.

2. Heat the olive oil in a large frying pan over medium-high heat. When the oil is nice and hot, transfer the marinated fillets to the pan, reserving the marinade for later. Fry the fillets for 3 minutes, before flipping the fish, and pouring the reserved marinade into the pan. Continue to fry the fish until completely opaque, about 3-4 additional minutes. Scrape the cooked fish onto a plate, and set aside.

3. Return the pan to the heat, and add the cauliflower rice. Stir for 5 minutes, or until the cauliflower is just cooked.

4. Scrape the cooked cauliflower rice onto a plate, and top with the cooked sea bass fillets. Garnish with spring onions, and serve hot.

Quick Tip:
Any leftovers can be refrigerated in an airtight container for no more than 4 days.

CURRIED HALIBUT & BROWN RICE

COOK TIME: 10-15 MINS | MAKES: 4 SERVINGS

INGREDIENTS:

- 1 tbsp. extra-virgin avocado oil
- 3 tbsp. green curry paste
- 13.5 oz. canned coconut milk
- 1 cup low-sodium chicken stock
- 1\8 tsp. Himalayan salt
- 1 1\2 lbs. skinless, de-boned halibut, cut into small cubes
- 1\3 cup fresh basil leaves, chopped
- 1 tbsp. freshly squeezed lemon juice
- 2 cups brown basmati rice, cooked, for serving

DIRECTIONS:

1. In a large frying pan over medium-high heat, heat the olive oil, before adding the curry paste, and frying for 30 seconds. Stir in the coconut milk, chicken stock, and half of the salt. When the sauce begins to simmer, reduce the heat to low, and simmer for 3 minutes while stirring, until the sauce begins to thicken.

2. Season the halibut with the remaining salt before adding it to the simmering sauce. Place the lid on the pot, and simmer for 6-8 minutes, or until the fish is cooked all the way through. Add the basil leaves and lemon juice, stirring to combine.

3. Serve the halibut on a bed of cooked brown basmati rice, with the curry sauce spooned over the fish.

LOBSTER & ANGEL HAIR PASTA

COOK TIME: 40 MINS | MAKES: 2 3 SERVINGS

INGREDIENTS:

- 1 tbsp. extra-virgin olive oil
- 1 whole bay leaf, torn
- 2 spring onions, diced
- 2 tsp. crushed garlic
- 1\4 cup carrots, chopped
- 1\4 cup celery, chopped
- 2 tsp. balsamic vinegar
- 1 cup coconut cream
- 1 1\2 cups store-bought chicken bone stock
- 1 lb. cooked lobster
- 7 oz. cooked angel hair pasta

DIRECTIONS:

1. In a large pot over medium heat, heat the oil. When the oil is nice and hot, fry the bay leaf, spring onions, garlic, carrots, and celery for 5 minutes. When the carrots are fork-tender, add the vinegar, and stir for 3 additional minutes.

2. Stir in the coconut cream and chicken bone stock over medium-high heat. When the stock begins to simmer, lower the heat to maintain a gentle simmer for 20 minutes, stirring occasionally to prevent burning. The sauce should begin to thicken during this time.

3. Add the lobster and cooked pasta, stirring to combine. With the heat on the lowest setting, simmer the pot for an extra ten minutes.

4. Spoon the pasta onto plates, and serve immediately.

Quick Tip:
Any leftovers can be refrigerated in an airtight container for no more than 4 days.

SIMPLE PESTO HALIBUT & SPROUTS

COOK TIME: 20 MINS | MAKES: 2 SERVINGS

INGREDIENTS:

- 2 boneless halibut fillets, skins removed
- Large pinch of kosher salt
- Small pinch of white pepper
- 2 tbsp. extra-virgin olive oil (divided)
- 2 tablespoons basil-olive pesto (divided)
- 1\2 lb. shredded Brussels sprouts

DIRECTIONS:

1. Cover a large, rimmed baking tray with grease-proof paper, and set the oven to preheat to 425°F, with the wire rack in the center of the oven.

2. Place the fillets on the prepared baking tray, and season with salt and pepper on both sides. Drizzle each fillet with 1\2 tablespoon of olive oil, massaging them as you go. Spread half of the pesto over the top of each fillet in an even layer.

3. Fan the shredded Brussels sprouts over half of the baking tray beside the fillets, and drizzle with the remaining olive oil. Season with salt and pepper.

4. Place the tray in the oven for 10 minutes, or until the edges of the fish are opaque, but the center is still raw. Use a spatula to flip the fish onto a serving platter. Spread the remaining pesto over the other side of the fillets, and tent to keep warm. The fish will continue to cook while you roast the sprouts.

5. Spread the sprouts out over the tray in an even layer, and bake for an additional 5-10 minutes, or until the edges of the sprouts become crispy.

6. Serve the cooked fish on a bed of crispy Brussels sprouts.

Quick Tip:
Any leftovers can be refrigerated in an airtight container for no more than 4 days.

ALMOND-SPICED MACKEREL & VEG

COOK TIME: 30-35 MINS | MAKES: 4 SERVINGS

INGREDIENTS:

- 1 medium butternut squash, peeled, and sliced into thin strips
- 3 1\2 cups chopped broccoli florets
- 2 large carrots, peeled, and thinly sliced
- 2 tbsp. extra-virgin avocado oil
- 1 1\2 tsp. Himalayan salt (divided)
- 1\4 tsp. freshly ground black pepper
- 1 tsp. garlic powder

- 3\4 cup almond flour
- 1\4 cup tapioca flour
- 1 tsp. dried dill
- 1\2 tsp. sweet smoked paprika
- 1 cup raw unsalted almonds
- 2 large eggs
- 4 mackerel fillets, patted dry
- 1 lemon, cut into 4 wedges

DIRECTIONS:

1. Cover a large, rimmed baking tray with tin foil, and set the oven to preheat to 425°F, with the wire rack in the center of the oven.

2. In a large mixing bowl, toss together the squash, broccoli, and carrots. Add the oil, 1 teaspoon of salt, pepper, and garlic powder, tossing until all of the vegetables are evenly coated. Fan the coated vegetable out in a single layer on the prepared baking tray. Place the tray in the oven for 20 minutes.

3. In a medium-sized mixing bowl, whisk together the almond flour, tapioca flour, dill, paprika, and the remaining 1\2 teaspoon of salt. Place the almonds in a high-speed blender, and process on high for 20-30 seconds, until the almonds resemble coarse sand. Scrape the almonds into a second mixing bowl. Lightly beat the eggs in a third mixing bowl.

4. After 20 minutes, remove the tray from the oven. Toss the vegetables, and push them to the side of the pan, making room for the fillets.

5. Line the three bowls up next to the baking tray, starting with the flour, and ending with the almonds. Begin by dredging 1 mackerel fillet in the flour, then the eggs, and finally the coarse almonds. Place the fillet on the baking tray, and repeat the process with the others. Strew any leftover almonds over the fillets, and gently press them into the coated fish.

6. Place the tray in the oven for 11-13 minutes, or until the fish flakes when poked with a fork, and the veggies are soft.

7. Serve immediately, with the lemon wedges on the side.

ZESTY SHRIMP SKEWER BOWLS

COOK TIME: 5 MINS | MAKES: 2 SERVINGS

INGREDIENTS:

- 1\8 tsp. kosher salt
- 1 tsp. crushed garlic
- 1 tbsp. coconut aminos
- 2 tbsp. freshly squeezed lemon juice
- 1 tbsp. extra-virgin olive oil
- 1\2 lb. shrimp, peeled and deveined
- 3 cups mixed salad greens
- 2 tbsp. coriander lime vinaigrette

DIRECTIONS:

1. In a medium-sized mixing bowl, whisk together the salt, garlic, coconut aminos, lemon juice, and olive oil. Place the shrimp in the bowl, and toss, making sure that they are all evenly coated. Cover with cling wrap, and chill for 25 minutes. Soak 6 bamboo skewers in warm water for 10 minutes.

2. Preheat the broiler, with the oven rack 4 inches away from the top, and line a rimmed baking tray with tin foil.

3. Divide the marinated shrimp, and thread them onto the 6 soaked skewers. Throw away the leftover marinade.

4. Arrange the skewers on the prepared baking tray, and broil in the oven for 5-6 minutes.

5. Divide the mixed salad greens between two serving bowls, and sprinkle with the coriander vinaigrette. Arrange three skewers in each bowl, and serve immediately.

Quick Tip:
Any leftovers can be refrigerated for no more than 4 days, in an airtight container.

GARLIC-SEARED SCALLOPS & SPINACH

COOK TIME: 15-20 MINS | MAKES: 4 SERVINGS

INGREDIENTS:

- 1\4 cup kosher salt (plus 1\2 tsp.)
- 7 cups lukewarm water
- 1 1\4 lbs. sea scallops
- 3 tbsp. ghee (divided)
- 1\2 cup vegetable stock
- 1 tbsp. lime juice
- 2 cups fresh spinach, stemmed and chopped
- 4 tsp. crushed garlic
- Fresh parsley, chopped, for garnish

DIRECTIONS:

1. In a large mixing bowl, whisk together the 1\4 cup of salt and 7 cups of water, until all of the salt granules have dissolved. Submerge the scallops in the saltwater, and soak for 10 minutes. Drain the water from the scallops, and pat each one dry with paper towels.

2. In a large frying pan over high heat, melt 1 tablespoon of ghee. When the ghee is nice and hot, arrange the scallops in the pan, and fry for 2-2 1\2 minutes, gently pressing the scallops into the bottom of the pan as they fry. Gently flip the scallops. The bottoms should be nicely toasted, with a brown crust. Add another tablespoon of ghee to the pan, and spoon the melted ghee over the scallops, while they cook for an additional 1-2 minutes. The scallops are done when an inserted meat thermometer reaches 145°F. Transfer the cooked scallops to a paper-towel-lined plate.

3. Reduce the heat to low, and pour the vegetable stock into the same pan used to fry the scallops. Stir the stock as it heats, scraping the bottom of the pan with a wooden spoon to remove any food that has stuck to the pan. Stir in the final tablespoon of ghee. When the ghee has melted, add the lime juice and spinach to the pan. Allow the spinach to cook while stirring, about 3-4 minutes. When the spinach begins to wilt, stir in the garlic and remaining salt. Stir, and allow the garlic to flavor the spinach for 1 minute.

4. Add the seared scallops back to the pan. Flip the scallops a few times in the sauce, until all of them are evenly coated.

5. Plate the scallops on a bed of cooked spinach, with the sauce spooned over everything. Garnish with parsley, and serve.

SAUCY GARLIC MUSSELS

COOK TIME: 35 MINS | MAKES: 2 SERVINGS

INGREDIENTS:

- 2 tsp. coconut oil
- 2 tsp. fresh ginger, grated
- 2 tsp. crushed garlic
- 1 shallot, thinly sliced
- 2 tsp. white wine vinegar
- Pinch of kosher salt
- 1 tbsp. fish sauce
- 2 tbsp. coconut aminos
- 2 2\3 cups full-fat, unsweetened coconut milk
- 2 lbs. fresh mussels, scrubbed
- 1\4 cup fresh coriander leaves, chopped
- 1 spring onion, finely chopped
- 2 AIP garlic herb flatbreads, sliced lengthwise into breadsticks

DIRECTIONS:

1. Melt the coconut oil in a large pot over medium heat. When the oil is nice and hot, add the ginger, garlic, and shallots. Fry and toss for 3-5 minutes, until the shallots become translucent. Stir in the vinegar for 2-3 additional minutes.

2. Add the salt, fish sauce, coconut aminos, and coconut milk to the pot, stirring to combine.

3. Stir the mussels into the pot, discarding any that have already opened. You should never try to cook already opened mussels. Place a lid on the pot, and cook the mussels for 5-7 minutes, discarding any that have not opened after several minutes. Unopened means inedible.

4. Spoon the cooked mussels into a large serving bowl, and stir in the chopped coriander leaves. Sprinkle with the spring onions, and serve with the bread on the side for optional dipping.

OVEN-BAKED CRAB, MUSHROOMS, & ASPARAGUS

COOK TIME: 20 MINS | MAKES: 2 SERVINGS

INGREDIENTS:

- 4 oz. lump or jumbo crab meat
- 2 tbsp. AIP mayonnaise
- 1\8 tsp. garlic powder
- 2 large Portobello mushrooms, stems and gills removed, and tops wiped clean
- Pinch kosher salt
- Freshly ground black pepper
- 2 tsp. extra-virgin olive oil (plus 1 tbsp.)
- 1\2 lb. asparagus spears, ends trimmed

DIRECTIONS:

1. Set the oven to preheat to 375°F, with the wire rack in the center of the oven.

2. Place the crab meat, mayonnaise, and garlic powder in a large mixing bowl. Using a wooden spoon, very gently fold all of the ingredients together, until the crab meat is evenly coated. You don't want to over-mix, as this will cause the meat to break apart.

3. Arrange the cleaned mushroom tops on one side of a tin foil-lined baking tray. Lightly sprinkle each mushroom with salt and pepper. Drizzle 1 teaspoon of oil over each seasoned cap. Spoon equal amounts of the crab mixture into each cap.

4. Arrange the asparagus spears on the other half of the tray. Sprinkle with the remaining oil, and season to taste with salt and pepper.

5. Place the tray in the oven for 2o minutes, or until the asparagus is fork-tender.

6. Plate the crab-stuffed mushrooms alongside the baked asparagus spears, and serve warm.

Quick Tip:
Any leftovers can be refrigerated in an airtight container for no more than 4 days.

HONEY-SOY SALMON & VEG

COOK TIME: 40 MINS | MAKES: 4 SERVINGS

INGREDIENTS:

- 2 tsp. crushed garlic
- 1 tbsp. freshly squeezed lemon juice
- 1 tbsp. raw wild honey
- 3 tbsp. extra-virgin olive oil
- 1 1\2 tablespoons gluten-free, lower-sodium soy sauce
- 4 skin-on salmon fillets
- 1 lb. yams, cut into 1\4-inch cubes
- 1\2 tsp. Himalayan salt (divided)
- 1\2 tsp. freshly ground black pepper (divided)
- 12 oz. fresh haricot verts, trimmed

DIRECTIONS:

1. Cover a large, rimmed sheet pan with tin foil. Coat the tin foil with a light layer of baking spray, and set the oven to preheat to 400°F, with the wire rack in the center of the oven.

2. In a large bowl, whisk together 1 teaspoon of garlic, the lemon juice, honey, 1 tablespoon of oil, and the soy sauce. Coat the salmon fillets in the marinade, and set aside in the marinade bowl.

3. Place the yam cubes on the prepared sheet pan, and toss with 1 tablespoon of oil, 1\4 teaspoon of salt, and 1\4 teaspoon of pepper. Place the sheet in the oven for 20-25 minutes, or until the yams just begin to soften.

4. In a medium-sized bowl, toss the haricot verts with the remaining oil, garlic, salt, and pepper. Add them to the pan of yams, and toss everything together. Push the vegetables to the side, making room for the salmon fillets.

5. Arrange the salmon fillets on half of the pan, discarding the remaining marinade. Place the pan back in the oven for 15 minutes, or until the vegetables are fork-tender, and the salmon is properly cooked.

6. Serve warm, and enjoy.

SIMPLE SHRIMP EGG ROLL BOWL

COOK TIME: 10-15 MINS | MAKES: 5 SERVINGS

INGREDIENTS:

- 2 tsp. raw wild honey
- 1 tbsp. rice vinegar
- 1 tsp. freshly squeezed lemon juice
- 1 tbsp. red chili paste
- 1\2 cup paleo mayonnaise
- 1 lime, juiced (divided)
- 1 lb. shrimp, peeled and deveined
- 1\2 tsp. kosher salt
- 2 tbsp. coconut oil (divided)
- 1 tsp. fresh ginger, grated
- 2 tsp. crushed garlic
- 1 tbsp. pure maple syrup
- 1\3 cup coconut aminos
- 1 lb. packaged mixed coleslaw
- 1\4 cup spring onions, chopped

DIRECTIONS:

1. In a small mixing bowl, whisk together the honey, rice vinegar, lemon juice, chili paste, and mayonnaise. Seal the bowl with cling wrap, and chill while you prepare the rest of the dish.

2. In a medium bowl, toss half of the lime juice with the shrimp and salt.

3. In a large frying pan over high heat, heat 1 tablespoon of the coconut oil. When the oil is nice and hot, toss the shrimp for about 4 minutes, until they blush, and the tails curl into a C. Scoop the cooked shrimp onto a paper-towel-lined plate. Discard any excess juices from the pan.

4. Reduce the heat to medium, and melt 1 tablespoon of coconut oil in the same pan used to fry the shrimp. When the oil is nice and hot, fry the ginger and garlic for 1-2 minutes until fragrant. Stir in the remaining lime juice, along with the maple syrup, coconut aminos, and coleslaw. Continuously stir the pan for 3-5 minutes, or until the coleslaw softens. Return the shrimp to the pan, and stir to combine. Add the spring onions, and toss for 1 minute.

5. Serve the shrimp and slaw drizzled with the chilled aioli.

STIR-FRIED FLOUNDER

COOK TIME: 10-15 MINS | MAKES: 4 SERVINGS

INGREDIENTS:

- 1\2 tsp. white pepper
- 1 1\2 tsp. toasted sesame oil
- 1 1\2 tsp. fresh ginger, minced
- 2 teaspoons gluten-free, lower-sodium soy sauce
- 1 tbsp. filtered water
- 2 tablespoons gluten-free hoisin sauce
- 2 1\2 tbsp. extra-virgin avocado oil
- 4 flounder fillets
- 6 oz. fresh sugar snap peas (1 store-bought bag)
- 2 spring onions, thinly sliced

DIRECTIONS:

1. In a medium-sized glass bowl, whisk together the pepper, sesame oil, ginger, soy sauce, water, and hoisin sauce. Transfer 4 teaspoons to a small glass bowl.

2. In a large frying pan over medium-high heat, heat 1 tablespoon of the avocado oil. When the oil is nice and hot, tilt the pan to cover the bottom. Add two of the fillets, and fry for 4 minutes before flipping. Use a basting brush to coat each fillet with 1 teaspoon of the reserved marinade. Fry the fish for an additional 2 minutes before transferring to a dish, and tenting to keep warm. Add 1 tablespoon of avocado oil to the pan, and repeat the steps with the remaining fillets and marinade.

3. Prepare the peas in the microwave by following the package instructions. Drain any excess water.

4. In a clean frying pan, heat the remaining 1\2 tablespoon of avocado oil. When the oil is nice and hot, fry the peas and spring onions for 3 minutes.

5. Serve the fillets on a bed of cooked peas and spring onions. Drizzle the marinade over the fish before serving.

DECONSTRUCTED SUSHI TUNA ROLLS

COOK TIME: 5 MINS | MAKES: 2 SERVINGS

INGREDIENTS:

- 2 tsp. fish sauce
- 2 tbsp. coconut aminos
- 2 tsp. fresh ginger, grated
- 2 tsp. crushed garlic
- 2 tuna steaks
- 2 tsp. wasabi paste
- 3 tablespoons AIP mayonnaise
- 1 large Hass avocado, pitted, peeled, and diced
- 1 English cucumber, chopped
- 1\2 English cucumber, diced
- 2 tbsp. coriander lime vinaigrette
- 1 tbsp. extra-virgin olive oil

DIRECTIONS:

1. In a large mixing bowl, whisk together the fish sauce, coconut aminos, ginger, and garlic. Coat the tuna steaks in the marinade, and leave them to soak in it. Cover the bowl with cling wrap, and chill for 25 minutes.

2. In a small glass bowl, whisk together the wasabi paste and mayonnaise. Chill while you prepare the rest of the dish.

3. In a medium-sized salad bowl, toss together the avocado, cucumbers, and vinaigrette. Chill for later.

4. In a large frying pan over high heat, heat the olive oil. When the oil is nice and hot, fry the tuna steaks for 2 minutes per side. The outside will cook while the inside remains pink.

5. Serve the pan-seared steaks alongside the chilled salad, with a dash of the wasabi mayo on the side.

CORIANDER-BUTTERED COD FILLETS

COOK TIME: 12 MINS | MAKES: 4 SERVINGS

INGREDIENTS:

- 4 cod fillets
- 1 teaspoon all-purpose taco seasoning
- Olive oil cooking spray
- 1 whole lemon, juiced
- 1\8 tsp. Himalayan salt
- 1\2 tsp. lemon zest
- 2 tbsp. fresh coriander leaves, finely chopped
- 1 tsp. crushed garlic
- 2 tbsp. butter, room temperature

DIRECTIONS:

1. Place the fillets on a wooden chopping board, and season both sides with the taco seasoning.

2. Coat a large frying pan with olive oil cooking spray before heating the pan over medium-high heat. Lightly coat the seasoned fillets with the spray, before adding them to the hot pan. Fry each fillet for 3 minutes per side, until the fish is cooked all the way through. Plate the fish before pouring the fresh lemon juice over the fillets.

3. In a small glass bowl, whisk together the salt, lemon zest coriander leaves, garlic, and butter.

4. Place a dollop of the coriander butter over each hot fish fillet, and serve.

SEAFOOD & CORIANDER SLAW TACOS

COOK TIME: 10-15 MINS | MAKES: 4 SERVINGS

INGREDIENTS:

- 1\4 cup fresh coriander leaves, chopped
- 1\3 cup spring onions, chopped
- 10 oz. store-bought angel hair coleslaw
- 2 tbsp. freshly squeezed lime juice
- 5 tsp. extra-virgin olive oil (divided)
- 1\2 tsp. Himalayan salt (divided)
- 1 lb. tilapia fillets
- 1 teaspoon all-purpose taco seasoning
- 8 corn taco shells, heated, for serving

DIRECTIONS:

1. In a large mixing bowl, toss together the coriander leaves, spring onions, coleslaw, lime juice, 3 teaspoons of oil, and 1\4 teaspoon of salt.

2. Place the tilapia fillets on a wooden chopping board, and season both sides with the taco seasoning and remaining 1\4 teaspoon of salt.

3. In a large frying pan over medium-high heat, heat the remaining 2 teaspoons of oil. When the oil is nice and hot, fry the fillets for 3 minutes per side, until the fish is opaque. Transfer the cooked fillets to a plate, and let cool slightly before slicing into strips.

4. Divide half of the slaw between the 8 taco shells. Top with the fish strips, followed by the rest of the slaw. Serve immediately.

SHRIMP-STUFFED SPAGHETTI SQUASH

COOK TIME: 40-45 MINS | MAKES: 4 SERVINGS

INGREDIENTS:

- 2 large spaghetti squash, halved and seeded
- 4 tbsp. extra-virgin avocado oil (divided)
- 1 1\2 tsp. Himalayan salt (divided)
- 1 lb. shrimp, peeled and deveined
- 4 tsp. crushed garlic (divided)

- 1\2 tsp. cayenne pepper
- 4 tbsp. ghee (divided)
- 1\2 lemon, juiced
- 1\3 cup chicken stock
- 2 tbsp. fresh parsley (more for garnish)

DIRECTIONS:

1. Cover a large, rimmed baking pan with greaseproof paper, and set the oven to preheat to 425°F, with the wire rack in the center of the oven.

2. Drizzle the inside of the squash halves with 2 tablespoons of the oil, before seasoning with 1 teaspoon of salt. Arrange the squash halves on the prepared baking pan, bottoms facing up. Place the pan in the oven for 25 minutes.

3. In a large mixing bowl, toss the shrimp with 1\2 teaspoon of salt, 1 tablespoon of oil, 2 teaspoons of garlic, and the cayenne pepper.

4. In a large frying pan over medium heat, heat the final tablespoon of oil. When the oil is nice and hot, toss the shrimp in the pan for about 4 minutes, or until they blush, and the tails curl into a C. Scrape the shrimp back into the bowl, and tent to keep warm.

5. Add 3 tablespoons of the ghee to the same pan over medium-low heat. When the ghee has melted, fry the rest of the garlic for 1-2 minutes. Pour the lemon juice and chicken stock into the pan, stirring for 5-6 minutes, and scraping the bottom of the pan to loosen any bits that may have stuck to it. The sauce should begin to thicken while you stir.

6. Stir in the shrimp, the remaining ghee, and two tablespoons of parsley. Taste the sauce, and add the remaining salt, if desired.

7. Once the squash is cooked, allow the halves to cool enough to be handled. Use a fork to twirl the insides of the squash, creating strands. Add the squash strands to the pan, and stir to combine all of the ingredients. Divide the contents of the pan between the empty squash boats. Return the pan with the filled squash boats to the oven, and bake for 8-10 minutes, until the tops are just beginning to crisp.

8. Serve the shrimp boats garnished with parsley.

POULTRY

PINE NUT GREMOLATA-TOPPED CHICKEN

COOK TIME: 8 MINS | MAKES: 4 SERVINGS

INGREDIENTS:

- 4 skinless, de-boned chicken breasts
- 1\2 tsp. Himalayan salt (divided)
- 1\4 tsp. white pepper (divided)
- 3 tbsp. extra-virgin avocado oil (divided)
- 1\3 cup fresh basil leaves
- 2 spring onions, chopped (green parts only)
- 1 1\2 tbsp. freshly squeezed lemon juice
- 1\3 cup lightly toasted pine nuts

DIRECTIONS:

1. Place the chicken breasts on a wooden chopping board, and use a wooden mallet to pound and flatten the breasts to about 3\4-inch thick. Season the breasts with half of the salt, and half of the pepper.

2. In a large frying pan over medium-high heat, heat 1 tablespoon of oil. When the oil is nice and hot, tilt the pan to spread the oil. Add the chicken breasts to the hot oil, and fry for 8 minutes, flipping halfway through the cooking time. The chicken should be properly cooked, and no longer pink in the middle. Transfer the cooked chicken to a plate.

3. In a blender, pulse the basil leaves, spring onions, lemon juice, pine nuts, and remaining salt and pepper, until you have a fine mixture. Drizzle in the rest of the oil, and pulse until all of the ingredients are properly combined.

4. Slice the chicken against the grain, and serve topped with the pine nut gremolata.

SIMPLE CHICKEN SHIRATAKI RICE

COOK TIME: 20 MINS | MAKES: 4 SERVINGS

INGREDIENTS:

- 7 oz. shirataki rice
- 1\2 cup ghee
- 1\3 cup cassava flour
- 1\2 cup celery, diced
- 1\2 cup carrots, diced
- 1\2 cup shallots, diced
- 1 tsp. crushed garlic
- 1 tsp. kosher salt
- 2 tsp. fresh thyme leaves, chopped
- 1 1\2 cups chicken stock
- 1 lb. chicken breasts, cooked and shredded

DIRECTIONS:

1. Cook the rice by following the package instructions, and set aside.

2. In a large frying pan over medium-low heat, melt the ghee. Gently whisk in the flour for 3-5 minutes. Keep an eye on the heat; the flour should not turn dark brown as you whisk.

3. Stir in the celery, carrots, shallots, and crushed garlic for about 5 minutes, or until the shallots become translucent, and the carrots soften. Add the salt, thyme, chicken stock, chicken, and cooked rice, stirring to combine. Raise the heat to medium, and simmer for 10 minutes, stirring occasionally to prevent burning.

4. Serve hot.

Quick Tip:
Any leftovers can be refrigerated for no more than 4 days in an airtight container, or frozen for 3 months.

SPINACH-SAUCED TURKEY MEATBALLS

COOK TIME: 25 MINS | MAKES: 4 SERVINGS

INGREDIENTS:

Meatballs:
- 1 lb. ground turkey
- 1\8 tsp. white pepper
- 1\2 tsp. Himalayan salt
- 1\2 tsp. onion powder
- 1\2 tsp. garlic powder
- 2 tsp. fresh rosemary, chopped
- 1 tbsp. fresh thyme, chopped
- 3 tbsp. fresh sage, chopped
- 2 tbsp. coconut flour
- 1\4 cup tapioca flour
- 1 large free-range egg
- 1 tbsp. extra-virgin olive oil

Spinach Sauce:
- 3 tbsp. coconut oil
- 1 tbsp. tapioca flour
- 2 1\2 cups chicken stock
- 1\2 tsp. Himalayan salt
- 1\4 tsp. white pepper
- 1 tbsp. French mustard
- 2 tbsp. coconut aminos
- 6 cups fresh baby spinach leaves
- Mashed potatoes for serving (optional)

DIRECTIONS:

1. In a large bowl, combine the turkey, pepper, salt, onion powder, garlic powder, rosemary, thyme, sage, coconut flour, tapioca flour, and egg. Use a wooden spoon to stir the ingredients until everything is properly combined. With a small ice cream scoop, or clean hands lightly dusted with coconut flour, form the mixture into 20 balls of roughly the same size.

2. In a deep-frying pan over medium heat, heat the olive oil. When the oil is nice and hot, fry the meatballs in batches for 3 minutes per side, until the meat is properly cooked, and the outside is nicely browned. Transfer the cooked meatballs to a paper-towel-lined bowl, and tent to keep warm.

3. Add the coconut oil to the same pan over medium-low heat. While the oil is melting, whisk the tapioca flour and chicken stock together in a large mixing bowl. Whisk the stock into the pan for 3-4 minutes, or until the sauce begins to thicken. Add the salt, pepper, mustard, and coconut aminos to the pan, whisking to combine. Stir in the spinach for a minute or two, or until the leaves wilt.

4. Add the meatballs to the sauce, and stir until they are all covered in sauce, and heated through.

5. Serve the meatballs and sauce on a bed of creamy mashed potatoes, if desired.

CRISPY CHICKEN & SLAW

COOK TIME: 40 MINS | MAKES: 4 SERVINGS

INGREDIENTS:

- 8 bone-in chicken thighs with the skin on
- 4 tbsp. extra-virgin olive oil
- 3 tsp. kosher salt (divided)
- 1 tsp. white pepper
- 1 tbsp. balsamic vinegar
- 2 tbsp. pure maple syrup
- 3 tbsp. coconut aminos
- 2 tbsp. coconut sugar
- 1\2 cup apple cider vinegar
- 14 oz. store-bought coleslaw mix

DIRECTIONS:

1. Set the oven to preheat to 425°F, with the wire rack in the center of the oven. Place a fitted wire rack over a large, rimmed baking sheet lined with tin foil.

2. Use paper towels to pat the thighs dry. Massage 2 tablespoons of the oil into the thighs, and season with 2 teaspoons of salt, and 1 teaspoon of pepper.

3. Arrange the seasoned thighs on the prepared wire rack over the baking tray, and bake in the oven for 35-40 minutes, or until the skin is nice and crispy, and the thighs are properly cooked.

4. In a small pot over medium heat, whisk together the balsamic vinegar, maple syrup, and coconut aminos. Once the sauce begins to simmer, reduce the heat to low, and maintain a gentle simmer for 10 minutes while stirring, or until the sauce thickens.

5. Meanwhile, in a medium-sized mixing bowl, whisk together the coconut sugar, apple cider vinegar, remaining salt, and 2 tablespoons of oil. Add the slaw to the bowl, and toss until all the slaw is evenly coated. Cover the bowl, and chill until the chicken is ready to be served.

6. If the chicken skin is not crisping up, place the tray under the broiler for 3-4 minutes to get a lovely crunch. When the chicken is done, baste the thighs with the juices from the pan, and serve alongside the chilled slaw.

Quick Tip:
Leftover chicken and slaw should be refrigerated in separate airtight containers for no more than 4 days, or frozen for up to 3 months.

CORIANDER & AVO CHICKEN TACOS

COOK TIME: 15 MINS | MAKES: 4 SERVINGS

INGREDIENTS:

- 1 lb. skinless, de-boned chicken breasts
- 3\8 tsp. Himalayan salt (divided)
- 2 teaspoons all-purpose taco seasoning
- 1\2 cup low-sodium chicken stock
- 2 tbsp. shallots, chopped
- 1 ripe avocado, chopped
- 1 cup cherry tomatoes, quartered
- 2 tsp. balsamic vinegar
- 1 tsp. extra-virgin olive oil
- 8 corn tacos, heated, for serving
- 1\4 cup crumbled feta cheese
- Fresh coriander leaves, chopped, for garnish

DIRECTIONS:

1. Season the chicken breasts with 1\4 teaspoon of salt, and the taco seasoning. Massage the spices into the meat.

2. In a medium-sized pot over medium heat, bring the stock and seasoned chicken breasts to a gentle boil. Reduce the heat to maintain a gentle simmer, and cook the chicken for 15 minutes with the lid on the pot, or until the chicken is properly cooked.

3. In a medium-sized bowl, toss together the shallots, avocados, and tomatoes. In a small glass bowl, whisk together the balsamic vinegar, remaining salt, and olive oil. Drizzle the vinegar over the salsa, tossing to coat. Chill for 1 hour.

4. When the chicken is done cooking, transfer to a wooden chopping board, and let cool for a few minutes. When the chicken is cool enough to handle, shred the breasts with a knife and fork.

5. Divide the shredded chicken between the heated tacos. Top with the chilled salsa, followed by the feta, and garnish with coriander leaves before serving.

CHICKEN PARM & SQUASH BAKE

COOK TIME: 60 MINS | MAKES: 6 SERVINGS

INGREDIENTS:

Casserole:
- 1 large spaghetti squash, halved and seeded
- 4 tbsp. extra-virgin olive oil (divided)
- 1\4 tsp. white pepper
- 1 tsp. Himalayan salt (divided)
- 1\2 medium shallot, diced
- 2 tsp. crushed garlic
- 2 cups sugar-free marinara sauce
- 1\2 tsp. cayenne pepper
- Fresh basil leaves, chopped, for garnish

Chicken:
- 1 lb. boneless chicken breasts, skins removed
- 2 large free-range eggs
- 1\4 tsp. freshly ground black pepper
- 1 tsp. Himalayan salt
- 1\3 tsp. Italian seasoning
- 1\3 cup tapioca flour
- 1 cup almond flour
- 1\4 cup coconut oil

DIRECTIONS:

1. Cover a large, rimmed baking tray with tin foil, and set the oven to preheat to 400°F.

2. Drizzle the insides of the spaghetti squash with 2 tablespoons of olive oil, and season with white pepper, and 1\2 teaspoon of salt. Arrange the squash halves on the prepared baking sheet with the bottoms facing up, and bake in the oven for 40 minutes, or until the flesh is tender.

3. While the squash halves bake, heat the remaining 2 tablespoons of olive oil in a large frying pan over medium heat. When the oil is nice and hot, fry the shallots and garlic for about 5 minutes or until the shallots soften. Scrape the cooked shallots and garlic into a small bowl, and set aside.

4. Place the chicken breasts on a wooden chopping board, and use a wooden mallet to pound the breasts to about 1\4-inch thick.

5. In a medium-sized bowl, lightly beat the eggs. In a separate bowl, whisk together the pepper, salt, Italian seasoning, tapioca flour, and almond flour. Working with one chicken breast at a time, dredge the breast in the flour, shaking off any excess. Dip the breast in the egg, before returning it to the flour for a second coating. Place the coated breast on a plate, and repeat the process with the remaining breasts.

6. In the same pan used to fry the shallots, melt the coconut oil over medium-high heat. When the oil is hot, fry the coated chicken breasts for 3 minutes per side, or until the chicken is properly cooked. Place the cooked chicken on a chopping board, and cut all the breasts into small pieces.

7. Once the squash halves are tender, remove the pan from the oven, and lower the heat to 375°F.

8. Scoop the insides of the cooked squash into a large baking dish. Add 1\2 teaspoon of salt, half of the marinara, the cooked shallots, and the cayenne pepper. Use a wooden spoon to stir all of the ingredients together, spreading the mixture over the bottom of the dish in an even layer.

9. Spread the remaining marinara sauce over the top. Arrange the chicken pieces on top of the sauce in an even layer.

10. Bake the dish in the oven for 30 minutes, or until the sauce is bubbling all the way through. Garnish with fresh basil leaves, and serve.

CRISPY DUCK & YAM MASH

COOK TIME: 25 MINS | MAKES: 4 SERVINGS

INGREDIENTS:

- 2 large yams, peeled and cubed
- 4 skin-on duck breast fillets
- Kosher salt
- 1 cup seedless red grapes
- 1\4 cup pure maple syrup
- 1\2 cup reserved duck fat
- 1\4 tsp. dried thyme
- Pinch of freshly ground black pepper

DIRECTIONS:

1. Set the oven to preheat to 400°F, with the wire rack in the center of the oven.

2. Place a large steamer basket or colander with a fitted lid over a pot of boiling water, the water should not be touching the bottom of the basket or colander. Place the yams in the basket or colander, and steam for 15-20 minutes, or until the yams are fork-tender.

3. Place the duck breasts on a wooden chopping board, and use a sharp knife to cut small Xs into the fat. Rub each breast with a small pinch of salt.

4. Heat a large, oven-safe frying pan over medium heat, and add the seasoned duck breasts to the pan, skin-side down. Fry the fillets for 6 minutes. Carefully scoop the fat from the pan into a small bowl, and reserve for later.

5. Carefully flip the breasts, and sear the other side for 1 minute, adding the grapes to the pan while the breasts sear. Flip the breasts back over, so that the skin is facing down once more. Bake the pan in the oven for 10 minutes, or until the duck is properly cooked. Remove the pan from the oven, and allow the duck to cool slightly before slicing into thin strips.

6. Meanwhile, add the cooked yams, a pinch of salt, the maple syrup, 1\2 cup reserved duck fat, thyme, and a pinch of pepper to a high-power blender. Pulse the yams until you have a smooth mash, and all of the ingredients are properly incorporated. You may need to stop halfway through, and push the mash back down.

7. Plate the cooked duck next to a serving of seasoned yam mash.

Quick Tip:
Any leftovers can be refrigerated in an airtight container for no more than 4 days.

CITRUS-BROILED GINGER CHICKEN

COOK TIME: 16 -18 MINS | MAKES: 4 SERVINGS

INGREDIENTS:

- 2 tsp. fresh ginger, finely chopped
- 2 tsp. crushed garlic
- 4 tsp. pure maple syrup
- 2 tablespoons gluten-free, lower-sodium soy sauce
- 2\3 cup freshly squeezed orange juice
- 2 tsp. freshly grated orange zest
- 2 oz. de-boned chicken thighs, skins removed

DIRECTIONS:

1. In a large mixing bowl, whisk together the ginger, garlic, syrup, soy sauce, orange juice, and orange zest. Coat the thighs in the orange marinade, and leave in it to soak. Cover the bowl with cling wrap, and chill for a minimum of 1 hour.

2. Line a large, rimmed baking tray with tin foil. Lightly coat the tin foil with baking spray. Preheat the oven broiler, with the wire rack in the center of the oven.

3. Arrange the marinated chicken thighs on the prepared baking tray, reserving the marinade for later. Broil the thighs for 16 minutes, turning halfway through the cooking time, or until the thighs are properly cooked.

4. Meanwhile, reheat the marinade in a small pot over medium-high heat. When the sauce begins to simmer, stir for 1 minute, or until the sauce begins to thicken.

5. Plate the chicken, and serve hot with the citrus sauce spooned over the top.

PORK-CRISPED CHICKEN FINGERS

COOK TIME: 20 MINS | MAKES: 4 SERVINGS

INGREDIENTS:

- 1 tsp. onion powder
- 1 tsp. garlic powder
- 1\4 cup arrowroot starch
- 1\2 cup cassava flour
- 1 1\2 cups crushed pork rinds
- 1 1\2 lbs. chicken tenders, cut in half lengthwise
- 1\2 tsp. dried rosemary
- 2 tbsp. coconut aminos
- 3 tbsp. pure maple syrup
- 6 cups mixed salad greens
- Himalayan salt
- Freshly ground black pepper

DIRECTIONS:

1. Cover a large, rimmed baking sheet with greaseproof paper, and set the oven to preheat to 375°F, with the wire rack in the center of the oven.

2. In a large mixing bowl, whisk together the onion powder, garlic powder, arrowroot starch, cassava flour, and crushed pork rinds. Add the chicken to the bowl, and toss until all of the pieces are evenly coated in the flour mixture.

3. Fan the coated chicken pieces out over the prepared baking pan, and bake in the oven for 20-25 minutes, or until the chicken is properly cooked, and the coating is crispy.

4. Meanwhile, in a small pot over medium-low heat, whisk together the rosemary, coconut aminos, and maple syrup. When the sauce begins to simmer, lower the heat to maintain a gentle simmer for 10 minutes, while stirring.

5. Serve the chicken fingers on a bed of mixed salad greens, drizzled with the sauce. Season to taste with salt and pepper before serving.

Quick Tip:
Any leftovers can be refrigerated in an airtight container for no more than 4 days.

CHEESY CHICKEN & CAULIFLOWER RICE

COOK TIME: 33 MINS | MAKES: 4 SERVINGS

INGREDIENTS:

- 2 tsp. extra-virgin olive oil
- 2 tsp. crushed garlic
- 1 small shallot, diced
- 4 cups broccoli florets
- 1 lb. boneless, skinless chicken breasts, cut into 1-inch cubes
- 2 cups cauliflower rice
- 1 1\2 cups store-bought cheese sauce

DIRECTIONS:

1. Set the oven to preheat to 350°F, with the wire rack in the center of the oven.

2. Heat the olive oil in a large, oven-safe frying pan over medium heat. When the oil is nice and hot, fry the garlic and shallots for 4-5 minutes, or until the shallots soften. Stir in the broccoli florets for an additional 5 minutes. Add the chicken cubes, and toss for 5 minutes, or until the chicken is properly cooked. Stir in the cauliflower rice for 2-3 minutes.

3. Pour the cheese sauce into the pan, and stir until everything is evenly coated, and the sauce is warm.

4. Transfer the pan to the oven, and bake for 15 minutes. Serve hot, and enjoy!

Quick Tip:
Any leftovers can be refrigerated in an airtight container for no more than 4 days, or frozen for up to 3 months.

BBQ CHICKEN-STUFFED ZUCCHINI

COOK TIME: 30 MINS | MAKES: 8 SERVINGS

INGREDIENTS:

- 4 medium zucchinis, halved lengthwise
- 1\2 tsp. Himalayan salt
- 1 tsp. garlic powder
- 1 tsp. onion powder
- 1 tbsp. sweet smoked paprika
- 1 tbsp. tomato paste
- 1 tbs. French mustard
- 3 tbsp. honey
- 1\3 cup apple cider vinegar
- 14.5 oz. canned tomato sauce
- 1 tbsp. extra-virgin olive oil
- 1\2 small shallot, diced
- 2 tsp. crushed garlic
- 1 lb. cooked rotisserie chicken, shredded

DIRECTIONS:

1. Set the oven to preheat to 400°F, with the wire rack in the center of the oven, and coat a large, rimmed baking tray with baking spray.

2. Remove the centers of the halved zucchinis, using a metal spoon, leaving about 1\2-inch of flesh right around the inside. Lightly coat the inside of the boats with baking spray.

3. In a small glass bowl, whisk together 1\2 teaspoon of salt, along with the garlic powder, onion powder, paprika, tomato paste, mustard, honey, apple cider vinegar, and tomato sauce.

4. Heat the olive oil in a large frying pan over medium heat. When the oil is nice and hot, add the shallots, and fry for 3-5 minutes, or until the shallots become translucent. Stir in the garlic, and continue to fry for an additional 1-2 minutes, allowing the flavors to meld. Scrape the cooked shallots and garlic into a large bowl, and stir in the chicken.

5. Scrape the BBQ sauce into the bowl of chicken, leaving about 3-4 tablespoons behind for later. Gently stir the chicken until the sauce is evenly distributed.

6. Scoop the chicken into the prepared zucchini halves in even amounts. Drizzle the remaining sauce over the chicken. Bake the tray in the oven for 20-25 minutes, or until the zucchini can easily be pierced with a fork.

7. Serve hot, and enjoy.

GINGER-FRIED CHICKEN QUINOA

COOK TIME: 10-15 MINS | MAKES: 2 SERVINGS

INGREDIENTS:

- 1 1\2 tbsp. extra-virgin olive oil
- 1\2 lb. deboned, skinless chicken thighs, cut into small pieces
- 1 tsp. fresh ginger, minced
- 2 tsp. crushed garlic
- 1\2 cup spring onions, chopped
- 1\2 cup red bell peppers, chopped
- 3\4 cup frozen shelled edamame beans, thawed
- 1\2 cup cooked quinoa, cooled
- 1 large free-range egg, lightly beaten
- 1/4 cup gluten-free, lower-sodium soy sauce

DIRECTIONS:

1. In a large frying pan over medium-high heat, heat 1 tablespoon of olive oil. When the oil is nice and hot, toss and fry the chicken for 4 minutes. Stir in the ginger, garlic, spring onions, and bell pepper for an additional 3 minutes, or until the chicken is properly cooked. Scrape the contents of the pan into a large bowl, and set aside.

2. Wipe the pan clean with a paper towel, and reduce the heat to medium. Heat the remaining olive oil. When the oil is nice and hot, fry the beans and quinoa for about 2 minutes, or until just heated through.

3. Push the quinoa and beans to the side of the pan. Fry and scramble the egg on the other side of the pan for about 1 minute, before mixing it through the quinoa. Scrape the chicken back into the pan, and add the soy sauce. Continue to stir everything for 1 minute, until the chicken is properly heated through.

4. Serve hot or cold.

Coriander-Topped Turkey Chili

COOK TIME: 30 MINS | MAKES: 6 SERVINGS

INGREDIENTS:

- 1 tbsp. extra-virgin avocado oil
- 1 red bell pepper, seeded and chopped
- 1 small shallot, seeded and chopped
- 1 lb. no-sugar-added Italian sausage, casings removed
- 1 lb. ground turkey
- 1 tsp. Himalayan salt
- 1\2 tsp. freshly ground black pepper
- 1 tsp. onion powder
- 1 tsp. garlic powder
- 1 tsp. ground cumin
- 2 tsp. coconut sugar
- 2 tsp. chili powder
- 2 tbsp. sweet smoked paprika
- 15 oz. canned tomato sauce
- 15 oz. canned sweet corn, drained
- 15 oz. canned black turtle beans, drained and rinsed
- 15 oz. canned diced tomatoes, drained
- chopped coriander for serving

DIRECTIONS:

1. In a large pot over medium heat, heat the avocado oil. When the oil is nice and hot, fry the red peppers and shallots for about 3 minutes, or until the shallots become translucent. Stir in the sausage and ground turkey, frying for 3-5 minutes, or until the meat is properly cooked, and no blood is visible.

2. Turn the heat up to medium-high, and stir in the salt, pepper, onion powder, garlic powder, cumin, coconut sugar, chili powder, paprika, tomato sauce, sweet corn, black beans, and diced tomatoes.

3. When the sauce begins to boil, lower the heat to maintain a gentle simmer for 20 minutes.

4. Serve the chili hot, garnished with coriander leaves.

CHICKEN MAYO-STUFFED YAMS

COOK TIME: 3-5 HOURS | MAKES: 6 SERVINGS

INGREDIENTS:

- 2 lbs. rotisserie chicken, deboned, and skin discarded
- 1 tsp. dried dill
- 1 tsp. garlic powder
- 1 cup canned coconut cream
- 1 cup paleo mayonnaise
- 6 medium yams, well-scrubbed
- 1 tsp. Himalayan salt
- 2 tbsp. extra-virgin olive oil
- Dairy-free ranch dressing for serving
- Fresh parsley leaves, chopped, for garnish

DIRECTIONS:

1. Chop the chicken into small cubes, and add it to a large slow cooker, along with the dill, garlic powder, coconut cream, and mayonnaise. Set the slow cooker to run for 3-4 hours on high, until the chicken is properly cooked. Stir a few times throughout the cooking process.

2. An hour before the chicken is done, set the oven to preheat to 425°F, with the wire rack in the center of the oven. Cover a large, rimmed baking tray with greaseproof paper.

3. Use a fork or sharp knife to poke holes all over the yam skins. Toss the yams in a large bowl with the salt and olive oil, until they are evenly coated. Arrange the seasoned yams on the prepared baking tray, and bake in the oven for 45-60 minutes, or until the yams soften. Allow them to cool on the counter for a few minutes.

4. Halve the cooked yams, and top each half with a generous dollop of the cooked chicken. Garnish with ranch dressing and parsley before serving.

SAUSAGE-STUFFED ACORN SQUASH

COOK TIME: 50-60 MINS | MAKES: 6 SERVINGS

INGREDIENTS:

- 3 medium acorn squash, halved, and seeds discarded
- 2 tbsp. extra-virgin olive oil
- 1 small shallot, chopped
- 3 tsp. crushed garlic
- 1 lb. no-sugar-added pork sausage, casings removed
- 1\2 tsp. Himalayan salt
- 1\4 tsp. freshly ground black pepper
- 2 tsp. fresh thyme, chopped
- 1 tbsp. fresh sage, chopped
- 1 tbsp. fresh rosemary, chopped
- 4 cups spinach, chopped
- 1 large apple, cored and chopped

DIRECTIONS:

1. Cover a large, rimmed baking pan with tin foil, and set the oven to preheat at 400°F, with the wire rack in the center of the oven.

2. Arrange the squash halves on the prepared baking pan with the bottoms facing up. Bake in the oven for 25-35 minutes, or until the shells begin to soften all the way through.

3. Meanwhile, heat the olive oil in a large frying pan over medium-low heat. When the oil is nice and hot, fry the shallots for 15-20 minutes, until all the pieces are nicely caramelized. Add the garlic, and stir for 1-2 minutes, allowing the flavors to meld.

4. Add the pork sausage, and turn the heat up to medium. Stir and cook the sausage for 6-8 minutes, or until all the meat has broken up. Stir in the salt, pepper, thyme, sage, rosemary, spinach, and apple, frying everything for a few more minutes, until the spinach begins to reduce in size.

5. Once the squash halves are soft, remove the pan from the oven, and turn on the broiler. Flip the squash in the pan, and fill each cup with a generous amount of the sausage mixture. Return the pan to the oven, and broil for 3-5 minutes, or until the tops are nice and crispy. Allow the cups to sit for a few minutes before serving.

ZESTY ORANGE & GINGER CHICKEN

COOK TIME: 28 MINS | MAKES: 4 SERVINGS

INGREDIENTS:

- 4 boneless, skinless chicken breasts, cut into 1-inch pieces
- 1\2 cup arrowroot starch
- 2 tsp. extra-virgin olive oil
- 1 tsp. fresh ginger, grated
- 2 tsp. crushed garlic
- 2 tbsp. coconut aminos
- 2 tbsp. apple cider vinegar
- 1\4 cup raw honey
- 1 cup freshly squeezed orange juice
- Zest of 1 orange
- 2 cups cauliflower rice
- 2 spring onions, chopped, for garnish

DIRECTIONS:

1. In a large bowl, toss the chicken pieces in the arrowroot starch, until all of the pieces are evenly coated.

2. Heat the olive oil in a large frying pan over medium heat. When the oil is nice and hot, fry the ginger and garlic for about 3 minutes, or until fragrant. Gently whisk in the coconut aminos, vinegar, honey, orange juice, and zest. Bring the sauce up to a gentle simmer, and whisk for 10 minutes.

3. Stir in the chicken, and cook for 15 minutes, or until the chicken is properly cooked, stirring throughout.

4. Meanwhile, steam the cauliflower rice in a steam basket over a pot of rapidly boiling water for 5 minutes, or until just softened. The water should not be touching the bottom of the basket.

5. Plate the cooked chicken on a bed of steamed cauliflower rice, with the sauce spooned over everything. Garnish with the spring onions before serving.

Quick Tip:
Any leftovers can be refrigerated in an airtight container for no more than 4 days, or frozen for 3 months.

CRANBERRY-GLAZED TURKEY FILLETS

COOK TIME: 20 MINS | MAKES: 4 SERVINGS

INGREDIENTS:

- 4 turkey fillets
- 1\4 tsp. garlic powder
- 1 tsp. kosher salt
- 1\4 cup coconut sugar
- 2 tbsp. balsamic vinegar
- 2 tbsp. freshly squeezed orange juice
- 2 tbsp. filtered water
- 2 tbsp. pure maple syrup
- 1 cup fresh cranberries
- Cauliflower mash, cooked, for serving

DIRECTIONS:

1. Cover a large, rimmed baking sheet with greaseproof paper, and set the oven to preheat to 400°F, with the wire rack in the center of the oven.

2. Place the turkey on the prepared baking sheet, and sprinkle all the fillets with the garlic powder and salt. Massage the spices into each fillet in an even layer. Bake in the oven for 20 minutes.

3. In a small pot over medium heat, whisk together the coconut sugar, vinegar, orange juice, water, syrup, and cranberries. Once the sauce begins to boil, stir the mixture for 10 minutes. Scrape the hot sauce into a high-powered food processor, and pulse on high until you have a lump-free sauce. You may want to place a kitchen towel over the top of the food processor before you pulse, as the sauce will be hot.

4. Plate the baked turkey fillets on a bed of cooked cauliflower mash, topped with the cranberry glaze. Serve hot.

Quick Tip:
Leftovers can be refrigerated in an airtight container for no more than 4 days.

BEEF, LAMB, & PORK

PULLED PORK & CORIANDER WRAPS

COOK TIME: 4-5 HOURS | MAKES: 8 SERVINGS

INGREDIENTS:

- 2 1\2 lbs. boneless pork shoulder, trimmed of excess fat
- 1\2 tsp. Himalayan salt
- 2 tbsp. all-purpose taco seasoning
- 2 tsp. extra-virgin avocado oil
- 2 cups chilled salsa (extra for serving)
- 16 corn tortillas
- 1 lime, sliced into wedges
- 1\2 cup fresh coriander leaves, chopped

DIRECTIONS:

1. Place the pork on a wooden chopping board, and slice the shoulder into 12 pieces of roughly the same size. Sprinkle the meat with the salt and taco seasoning, toss and massage the spices into the meat in an even layer.

2. Place the seasoned pork in a large slow cooker, along with the avocado oil, and 2 cups of salsa. Cook the pork on high for 4-5 hours, or until it is falling apart, and can easily be shredded.

3. When the pork is properly cooked, heat the corn wraps according to package instructions.

4. Once the pork has cooled slightly, place the meat on a chopping board, and shred into fine pieces.

5. Divide the shredded pork between the heated wraps, and top with extra salsa, a few squeezes of lime juice, fresh coriander leaves, and a few teaspoons of the slow cooker juices.

6. Serve hot, and enjoy.

BEEF BARBACOA BOWLS

COOK TIME: 10-11 HOURS | MAKES: 4 SERVINGS

INGREDIENTS:

- 1\4 cup paleo mayonnaise
- 1 tbsp. sriracha sauce
- 2 tsp. freshly squeezed lime juice
- 2 tbsp. extra-virgin olive oil
- 2 lbs. chuck roast
- 1 tsp. Himalayan salt
- 1\2 tsp. white pepper
- 1 tsp. toasted sesame oil
- 1 tbsp. raw wild honey
- 1\2 cup coconut aminos
- 1\4 cup beef stock
- 1 tbsp. fresh ginger, grated

- 3 tsp. crushed garlic
- 1 medium shallot, thinly sliced
- 2 tbsp. tapioca flour
- 4 cups basmati rice, cooked, for serving
- 1 cup kimchi
- 2 Hass avocados, peeled, pitted, and sliced
- 1\2 cup cucumbers, pitted, and sliced
- 1 cup red onions, sliced
- Fresh coriander leaves, chopped, for garnish
- Spring onions, chopped, for garnish
- Toasted sesame seeds, for garnish

DIRECTIONS:

1. In a small glass bowl, whisk together the mayonnaise, sriracha sauce, and lime juice. Seal the bowl with cling wrap, and chill for later.

2. In a large frying pan over high heat, heat the oil. Place the chuck roast on a wooden chopping board, and season with salt and pepper. When the oil is nice and hot, fry the chuck for 3-4 minutes per side, on all sides. When all the sides are properly seared, transfer the chuck to a large slow-cooker. To the slow cooker, add the sesame oil, honey, coconut aminos, beef stock, ginger, garlic, and shallots, stirring to combine. Cook on low for 10 hours, with the lid on the slow-cooker.

3. Use a sharp knife to shred the cooked beef. Spoon about 2 tablespoons of the slow-cooker stock into a small bowl, and whisk in the tapioca flour. Add the mixture back to the slow cooker, and gently whisk the stock to combine. Turn the cooker up to high, and cook with the lid on the pot for an additional 20 minutes, or until the stock thickens.

4. Divide the cooked rice between 4 serving bowls. Top the rice with layers of cooked beef, kimchi, avocados, cucumbers, and red onions. Garnish the bowls with coriander leaves, spring onions, and toasted sesame seeds. Place a dollop of the chilled mayo on each helping, and serve.

HONEY-ROASTED CARROTS & CHOPS

COOK TIME: 45 MINS | MAKES: 4 SERVINGS

INGREDIENTS:

- 1 1\2 tsp. kosher salt (divided)
- 3 tbsp. fresh rosemary, finely chopped (divided)
- 1 tbsp. raw wild honey
- 2 tbsp. extra-virgin olive oil (divided)
- 1 lb. baby carrots
- 12 lamb rib chops
- 1\4 tsp. garlic powder

DIRECTIONS:

1. Cover a large, rimmed baking sheet with greaseproof paper, and set the oven to preheat to 400°F, with the wire rack 4-5 inches away from the broiler. Place a second wire rack in the center of the oven.

2. In a large bowl, whisk together 1\2 teaspoon of salt, 1 tablespoon of rosemary, the honey, and 1 tablespoon of olive oil. Add the baby carrots, and toss until they are all evenly coated. Fan the coated carrots out on the prepared baking sheet, pouring any extra sauce over them. Bake in the oven, on the middle rack, for 35-40 minutes, or until the carrots are soft.

3. Massage the remaining olive oil into the chops, and season with the remaining salt, the remaining rosemary, and the garlic powder. Lightly coat a baking tray with olive oil spray, and preheat the broiler. Arrange the seasoned chops on the tray, and broil in the oven for 4 minutes, flipping halfway through the cooking time. The chops should be cooked all the way through.

4. Serve the lamb chops hot, with the baby carrots on the side.

BEEFY SHEPHERD'S PIE & VEG

COOK TIME: 60 MINS | MAKES: 6-8 SERVINGS

INGREDIENTS:

Ground beef and veg:
- 2 tbsp. extra-virgin olive oil
- 1 small shallot, chopped
- 2 tsp. crushed garlic
- 8 oz. button mushrooms, sliced
- 2 carrots, peeled and chopped
- 2 celery stalks, chopped
- 1 lb. ground beef
- 1 tsp. Himalayan salt
- 1\4 tsp. white pepper
- 1 cup frozen peas
- 2 tbsp. coconut aminos
- 2 tbsp. tomato paste
- 1 1\2 cups beef stock
- 14.5 oz. canned diced fire-roasted tomatoes with

the juices
- 2 tbsp. tapioca flour
- 2 whole bay leaves
- 3 sprigs fresh thyme
- 1 sprig fresh rosemary

Mash:
- 2 lbs. russet potatoes, peeled and cubed
- 1\2 cup coconut cream
- 1\4 cup almond milk
- 1\4 cup coconut oil
- 1 tsp. Himalayan salt
- 1\4 tsp. freshly ground black pepper
- 1\4 tsp. baking powder
- 1 tbsp. extra-virgin avocado oil

DIRECTIONS:

1. Set the oven to preheat to 350°F, with the wire rack in the center of the oven.

2. In a large, oven-safe, cast-iron frying pan, heat the olive oil over medium heat. When the oil is nice and hot, fry the shallots for 2-3 minutes, or until they are tender. Stir in the garlic for 1-2 minutes, allowing the flavors to meld. Add the mushrooms, carrots, and celery, frying and tossing for 4-5 minutes, until the carrots soften, and the mushrooms darken in color.

3. Stir in the ground beef, salt, and pepper. Raise the heat to high, and fry the beef for 4-5 minutes, or until properly cooked. If there is too much oil in the pan after frying the meat, throw off any excess. Turn the heat back down to medium, and stir in the peas, coconut aminos, tomato paste, beef stock, and canned tomatoes, along with their juices.

4. Spoon 2 tablespoons of the sauce into a glass bowl, and whisk in the tapioca flour. Gently whisk the mixture through the sauce. Add the bay leaves, thyme, and rosemary. Stir the sauce for 5 minutes over medium-low, or until the sauce thickens. Once the sauce thickens, remove and discard the fresh herbs. Transfer the pan to a wooden chopping board to cool while you prepare the rest of the dish. Allowing the ground beef and veg to cool to room temperature will ensure a more visible layer between the potatoes and meat.

5. Cover the potatoes with water in a large pot, and bring to a boil over medium-high heat. Boil the potatoes for 5-8 minutes, or until they soften. Drain the cooked potatoes in a colander. Transfer the potatoes to a large mixing bowl, and stir in the coconut cream, almond milk, coconut oil, salt, pepper, and baking powder. Use a potato masher or fork to mash the potatoes into fluffy, white clouds.

6. Carefully spoon the mash over the cooled meat in the pan, and smooth out the top. Push the mash as close to the edges of the pan as you can. Create a pattern on the top of the mash using a fork, or leave as is, before drizzling the top with the optional oil. Place the pan in the oven for 15-20 minutes, or until the meat layer is heated through, and the top is lightly browned. You may use the broiler for the final 3-5 minutes, to achieve the desired crispness on the top of the potatoes.

7. Allow the pie to cool for a few minutes before serving.

HEART SMART LAMB WRAPS

COOK TIME: 5-10 MINS | MAKES: 4 SERVINGS

INGREDIENTS:

- 1 tbsp. extra-virgin avocado oil
- 3 tsp. crushed garlic
- 1 cups shallots, finely chopped
- 12 oz. lean ground lamb
- 1 tsp. ground cinnamon
- 3\4 tsp. Himalayan salt
- 1\4 tsp. white pepper
- 1 cup English cucumber, chopped
- 1 cup cherry tomatoes, quartered
- 12 whole Boston lettuce leaves
- 3\4 cup refrigerated Greek yogurt tzatziki, or cucumber-dill dip

DIRECTIONS:

1. In a large frying pan over high heat, heat the avocado oil. When the oil is nice and hot, fry the garlic, shallots, lamb, cinnamon, salt, and pepper for about 5 minutes, or until the lamb is properly cooked.

2. When the lamb is cooked, stir in the cucumber and tomatoes. Divide the lamb between the lettuce leaves, and top with tzatziki or dip before folding and serving.

BEEF & BAKED GARLIC MUSHROOMS

COOK TIME: 30 MINS | MAKES: 4 SERVINGS

INGREDIENTS:

Beef:
- 1 1\4 lbs. boneless beef tenderloin, at room temperature
- 1 tbsp. extra-virgin olive oil
- 2 tsp. kosher salt
- 1\2 tsp. white pepper
- 1\2 tsp. crushed dried thyme
- 1\2 tsp. garlic powder

Mushrooms:
- 1 lb. button mushrooms, cleaned
- 2 tbsp. extra-virgin olive oil
- 3\4 tsp. kosher salt
- 1\4 tsp. white pepper
- 1 tsp. garlic powder
- 1 tsp. dried thyme

DIRECTIONS:

1. Set the oven to preheat to 425°F, with the wire rack in the center of the oven.

2. Place the beef tenderloin on a wooden chopping board, and drizzle with the oil. Season with the salt, pepper, thyme, and garlic powder, rubbing the spices into the meat. Heat a large, oven-safe frying pan over high heat, and sear the meat for 2 minutes per side, to seal in the juices.

3. Place the pan in the oven for 25 minutes for medium-rare. Transfer the pan to a wooden chopping board, and tent with foil to keep warm. The meat will continue to cook while you prepare the rest of the dish.

4. In a large bowl, toss the mushrooms with the oil, salt, pepper, garlic powder, and thyme, until all of the mushrooms are evenly coated. Transfer the beef to a serving platter, and tent with foil to keep warm. Fan the seasoned mushrooms out in the pan, and bake in the oven for 15 minutes, until the mushrooms darken, and release their juices. Shake the pan at regular intervals to prevent burning.

5. Slice the beef, and serve alongside the cooked mushrooms.

HONEYED MONGOLIAN PRESSURE COOKER BEEF

COOK TIME: 15-20 MINS | MAKES: 6-8 SERVINGS

INGREDIENTS:

- 1 tsp. fresh ginger, grated
- 4 tsp. crushed garlic
- 1\3 cup coconut aminos
- 1\2 cup filtered water
- 1 1\2 lbs. flank steak, thinly sliced against the grain
- 1 tbsp. tapioca flour
- 1\4 cup wild raw honey
- 2 cups chopped broccoli florets
- Brown basmati rice, cooked, for serving
- Toasted sesame seeds, for garnish
- Chopped spring onions, for garnish

DIRECTIONS:

1. Whisk the ginger, garlic, coconut aminos, and water together in a medium-sized bowl.

2. With your pressure cooker preheated on sauté, sear the steak for 20 seconds per side. Switch off the sauté option, and pour the ginger mixture over the steak. Seal the cooker, and cook on manual for 11 minutes.

3. After 11 minutes, release the steam, taking care not to burn yourself. Spoon two tablespoons of the sauce into a small glass bowl, and whisk in the flour. Gently whisk the mixture back into the cooker before stirring in the honey. Add the broccoli florets, and set the cooker back to sauté. Cook for an additional 5 minutes, or until the sauce thickens.

4. Plate the cooked beef and sauce on a bed of cooked rice. Garnish with the toasted sesame seeds and spring onions before serving.

SHIRATAKI RICE & PORK BALLS

COOK TIME: 20 MINS | MAKES: 4 SERVINGS

INGREDIENTS:

- 1 lb. ground pork
- 1 small shallot, grated
- 1 tsp. crushed garlic
- 1 tsp. fresh ginger, grated
- 1 tsp. kosher salt
- 1\4 tsp. white pepper
- 5 tbsp. coconut aminos (divided)
- 2 1\2 tbsp. fish sauce (divided)
- 2 tbsp. raw wild honey
- 14 oz. cooked shirataki rice, for serving

DIRECTIONS:

1. Line a large, rimmed baking sheet with greaseproof paper, and set the oven to preheat to 400°F, with the wire rack in the center of the oven.

2. Stir together the pork, shallots, garlic, ginger, salt, pepper, 1 tablespoon of coconut aminos, and 1\2 tablespoon of fish sauce in a large bowl. Use your hands to form the mixture into balls of about 1 1\2-inches thick. Arrange the balls in the prepared baking sheet, and bake in the oven for 15-20 minutes, or until the balls are cooked through, and the outsides are lightly toasted.

3. Meanwhile, in a small pot over medium-low heat, whisk together the remaining coconut aminos and fish sauce, along with the honey. When the sauce reaches a gentle simmer, lower the heat, and cook while stirring for 10 minutes.

4. When the pork balls are cooked, toss them in the sauce until they are evenly coated. Serve the pork balls and sauce on a bed of cooked shirataki rice.

Quick Tip:
Any leftovers can be refrigerated in an airtight container for no more than 4 days.

SWEET & SAVORY PINEAPPLE PORK

COOK TIME: 30 MINS | MAKES: 4 SERVINGS

INGREDIENTS:

- 2 tsp. fresh ginger, grated
- 2 tsp. crushed garlic
- 1\2 cup coconut aminos
- 1\4 cup extra-virgin avocado oil
- 1 lb. boneless pork tenderloin
- 1 tsp. kosher salt
- 1\4 cup filtered water
- 15-20 oz. canned pineapple slices packed in 100-percent pineapple juice, drained

DIRECTIONS:

1. In a medium-sized glass bowl, whisk together the ginger, garlic, coconut aminos, and avocado oil. Massage the tenderloin with the salt before submerging it in the bowl of marinade. Seal the bowl with cling wrap, and chill for a minimum of 4 hours.

2. Cover a large, rimmed baking tray with tin foil, and set the oven to preheat to 425°F, with the wire rack in the center of the oven.

3. Once the pork is properly chilled, transfer the meat to the prepared baking tray, and bake in the oven for 25 minutes, or until the pork is medium-rare. Reserve the marinade for later.

4. In a small pot over medium heat, whisk together the marinade from the pork, and the filtered water. When the sauce begins to boil, continuously whisk for 5 minutes, before lowering the heat to low, and simmering for an additional 5 minutes while you whisk.

5. When the meat is done, transfer it to a wooden chopping board, and allow to cool. Turn on the broiler, and place a wire rack 4-5 inches away from the top.

6. Arrange the pineapple slices on the same sheet used to bake the pork, and broil in the oven for 3-5 minutes.

7. When the pineapples are ready, and the pork has cooled slightly, slice the pork, and serve alongside the broiled pineapples, with the sauce spooned over everything.

Quick Tip:
Any leftovers can be refrigerated in an airtight container for no more than 4 days.

VEGETARIAN MAINS

VEG & TEMPEH KEBABS

COOK TIME: 30 MINS | MAKES: 4 SERVINGS

INGREDIENTS:

- garlic & herb marinated tempeh
- 8 bamboo kebab skewers
- 14 0z. brown basmati rice, cooked for serving
- 8 oz. button mushrooms, cleaned
- 1 red bell pepper, cut into large chunks
- 1 yellow squash, cubed (1\2-inch cubes)
- 1 small zucchini, sliced (1\2-inch-thick slices)
- 1 red onion, cut into large chunks

DIRECTIONS:

1. Follow package instructions to marinate the tempeh for at least 20 minutes.

2. Submerge the bamboo skewers in warm water for 8-10 minutes to prevent charring.

3. Prepare the rice according to package instructions.

4. Cover a large, rimmed baking sheet with greaseproof paper, and set the oven to preheat to 425°F, with the wire rack in the center of the oven.

5. Divide the marinated tempeh and veg between the skewers, threading everything in alternating patterns. You should leave about 1-inch of skewer visible on each side for handling. Keep the marinade for later.

6. Arrange the kebabs on the prepared baking sheet, and use a basting brush to coat the tempeh and veg with half of the marinade. Bake in the oven for 20 minutes, before flipping, and basting with the remaining marinade. Bake the other side of the skewers for 15-20 minutes, or until the vegetables are fork-tender, and the edges are crispy.

7. Drain the rice.

8. Divide the rice between 4 bowls, and top each bowl with 2 tempeh kebabs. Serve hot, and enjoy.

Quick Tip:
Roasted vegetables do not freeze well. Any leftovers should be refrigerated in an airtight container for no more than 5 days.

MANGO & BEAN LETTUCE WRAPS

COOK TIME: 5-10 MINS | MAKES: 4 SERVINGS

INGREDIENTS:

- 1 can black turtle beans, drained
- 2 tsp. crushed garlic
- 1 lime, juiced
- 1 tsp. extra-virgin olive oil
- 1\4 tsp. Himalayan salt
- 3\4 cup fresh coriander leaves, chopped
- 2 spring onions, thinly sliced
- 1 fresh mango, peeled and chopped
- 12 large butter lettuce leaves
- 1\2 cups mashed avocado

DIRECTIONS:

1. Heat the beans on the stove, or microwave in a microwave-safe dish. When the beans are hot, stir in the crushed garlic, and set aside.

2. In a medium-sized glass bowl, whisk together the lime juice, olive oil, salt, coriander leaves, and spring onions. Stir in the chopped mango.

3. Open each lettuce leaf, and spread the mashed avocado on the inside of each leaf, in even amounts. Top the avocado with beans, and the mango relish.

4. Fold, and serve immediately.

THAI-STYLE ZUCCHINI NOODLES

COOK TIME: 15-20 MINS | MAKES: 4 SERVINGS

INGREDIENTS:

- 2 tbsp. toasted sesame oil (divided)
- 1 cup red bell peppers, thinly sliced
- 6 cups thick spiralized zucchini noodles
- 1\2 tsp. Himalayan salt (divided)
- 3 cups fresh Swiss chard, chopped
- 8 oz. extra-firm tempeh, cut into 1/2-inch cubes
- 2 tbsp. yellow curry paste
- 3 tbsp. almond butter
- 1\4 cup filtered water
- 1\2 cup canned light coconut milk
- 1\4 cup unsalted cashews, chopped
- 1 lime, quartered

DIRECTIONS:

1. Heat 1 tablespoon of sesame oil in a large frying pan over medium-high heat. When the oil is nice and hot, fry the bell peppers for 4 minutes. Add the zucchini spirals, and season with 1\4 teaspoon of salt. Place a lid on the pan, and fry for 2 minutes. Stir in the chard, and cook for a few minutes, until the leaves reduce in size.

2. Scrape the noodles and chard into a large bowl, and set aside.

3. In the same pan, heat the last tablespoon of sesame oil. When the oil is nice and hot, fry the tempeh while stirring for 4 minutes. Remove the pan from the heat.

4. In a medium-sized bowl, whisk together the curry paste, almond butter, filtered water, and coconut milk. Pour the sauce over the cooked zucchini noodles, and toss until all of the noodles are evenly coated.

5. Scoop the noodles into 4 serving bowls, and drizzle with the sauce from the bottom of the mixing bowl. Place the fried tempeh over the noodles, and garnish with the toasted cashews. Drizzle with lime juice before serving.

SPROUTS & CHICKPEA SALAD

COOK TIME: 0 MINS | MAKES: 8-10 SERVINGS

INGREDIENTS:

Chickpeas:
- 1\2 tsp. cayenne pepper
- 1\2 tsp. Himalayan salt
- 1 tsp. fresh oregano, chopped
- 1 tsp. fresh thyme, chopped
- 1\3 cup extra-virgin olive oil
- 15 oz. canned chickpeas, drained and rinsed

Salad:
- 1\2 medium red onion, sliced
- 1 medium avocado, peeled, pitted, and sliced
- 1\2 cup black olives, halved
- 1 cup cherry tomatoes, quartered
- 2 cups English cucumber, diced
- 1 1\2 lbs. Brussels sprouts, grated

Dressing:
- 1\4 tsp. white pepper
- 1\2 tsp. Himalayan salt
- 1 tsp. fresh oregano, chopped
- 1 tbsp. fresh flat-leaf parsley, chopped
- 1 tsp. crushed garlic
- 2 tsp. paleo mayonnaise
- 1 small shallot, diced
- 1 tsp. French mustard
- 1 tbsp. lime juice, freshly squeezed
- 3 tbsp. balsamic vinegar
- 1\4 cup extra-virgin olive oil

DIRECTIONS:

1. In a medium-sized bowl, whisk together the cayenne pepper, salt, oregano, thyme, and olive oil. Stir in the chickpeas, and let stand for 10 minutes.

2. In a large bowl, toss together the red onion, avocado, olives, tomatoes, cucumbers, and Brussels sprouts.

3. Use a slotted spoon to transfer the marinated chickpeas to the bowl of salad, leaving the marinade behind. Toss the salad once more, to distribute the chickpeas.

4. Into the bowl of marinade, whisk in the pepper, salt, oregano, parsley, garlic, mayonnaise, shallots, mustard, lime juice, vinegar, and olive oil.

5. Drizzle the dressing over the salad, and toss to coat, before serving immediately.

GARLIC TOFU & AVOCADO WRAPS

COOK TIME: 0 MINS | MAKES: 4 SERVINGS

INGREDIENTS:

- Garlic & herb marinated tofu
- 4 large corn wraps
- 4 large butter lettuce leaves
- 1 cup store-bought zesty vegan Caesar dressing
- 2 medium carrots, thinly sliced
- 1 cup fresh bean sprouts
- 2 Hass avocados, pitted and sliced
- Himalayan salt
- Freshly ground black pepper

DIRECTIONS:

1. Follow the package instructions to marinate the tofu for at least 20 minutes.

2. Place the wraps on a clean counter. Place one lettuce leaf on each wrap, and spread 1\4 cup of dressing over all the leaves. Divide the carrots, beans, and marinated tofu between the wraps. Drizzle 1\2 cup of dressing over all the wraps, and top with the avocado slices.

3. Season the avocado slices with salt and pepper to taste, before dividing the rest of the dressing between the wraps.

4. Fold, and serve the wraps straight away.

Quick Tip:
For a warm wrap, microwave the tofu on high for 1 minute before building the wraps.

TAHINI-DRESSED LENTIL SALAD

COOK TIME: 40 MINS | MAKES: 2 SERVINGS

INGREDIENTS:

Salad:
- 3\4 cup green lentils, rinsed
- 8 medium carrots, peeled, and halved lengthwise
- 1 tbsp. extra-virgin avocado oil
- 1\2 tsp. Himalayan salt
- 1\4 tsp. white pepper
- 1 tsp. sweet smoked paprika
- 2 cups fresh baby spinach
- Fresh dill, chopped, for garnish

Tahini dressing:
- 2 tsp. raw wild honey
- 1\4 tsp Himalayan salt
- 1 tsp. crushed garlic
- 1\2 cup extra-virgin olive oil
- 2 tbsp. red wine vinegar
- 3 tbsp. tahini sauce
- Lightly toasted almond slices for serving

DIRECTIONS:

1. Set the oven to preheat to 425°F, with the wire rack in the center of the oven. Cover a large, rimmed baking sheet with tin foil.

2. In a medium-sized pot, bring the lentils to a boil over high heat, with just enough water to cover them. Once the water begins to boil, reduce the heat to medium-low, and simmer uncovered for 15-20 minutes, or until the lentils are cooked. Strain off the water, and set the lentils aside to cool.

3. In a large bowl, toss the carrots with the avocado oil, salt, pepper, and paprika. Fan the seasoned carrots out on the prepared baking sheet, and bake in the oven for 22-24 minutes, flipping halfway through the cooking process. The carrots are done when the centers are soft, and the outsides are nicely crisped.

4. In a medium-sized glass bowl, whisk together the honey, salt, crushed garlic, olive oil, red wine vinegar, and tahini sauce.

5. Divide the baby spinach between two serving bowls, and top with the cooked lentils and baked carrots. Garnish the bowls with the almond slices and chopped dilled, before drizzling the salads with the tahini dressing.

6. Serve immediately.

NUTTY STIR-FRIED BOK CHOY

COOK TIME: 10-15 MINS | MAKES: 4 SERVINGS

INGREDIENTS:

- 2 tsp. toasted sesame oil
- 1\2 small shallot, diced
- 1\2 tsp. fresh ginger, grated
- 1 tsp. crushed garlic
- 6 cups thinly sliced bok choy
- 2 tbsp. gluten-free, lower-sodium soy sauce
- 1\2 tsp. Himalayan salt
- 1\4 tsp white pepper
- 1\8 tsp. cayenne pepper (optional)
- 1\4 cup raw, unsalted cashews

DIRECTIONS:

1. In a large frying pan over medium-high heat, heat 1 teaspoon of the oil. When the oil is nice and hot, fry the shallots for 3-5 minutes, or until they become transparent. Stir in the ginger and garlic, and fry for 1-2 minutes, allowing the flavors to meld.

2. Add the bok choy to the pan, and fry for 2-3 minutes, or until the leaves reduce in size, and the edges become crispy. Scrape the cooked bok choy into a large bowl. If all of the Bok choy does not comfortably fit in the pan, fry it in batches using the extra sesame oil.

3. Toss the cooked bok choy with the soy sauce, salt, pepper, and optional cayenne pepper.

4. Divide the bok choy between 4 serving bowls, and garnish with the cashews before serving.

SWEET & TANGY APPLE QUINOA

COOK TIME: 15 MINS | MAKES: 4 SERVINGS

INGREDIENTS:

- 14 oz. extra-firm tempeh
- 2 cups filtered water
- 1 cup wild quinoa, rinsed
- 1 tsp. raw wild honey
- 2 tsp. French mustard
- 1\2 tsp. kosher salt
- 1\2 tsp. freshly ground black pepper
- 1\4 cup apple cider vinegar
- 1\3 cup extra-virgin olive oil
- 3 cups baby arugula, chopped
- 1 medium apple, chopped

DIRECTIONS:

1. Place the tempeh strips on 6 paper towels, and cover with 6 additional paper towels. Place a heavy book or pot over the tempeh to press out any extra water. Once the tempeh is properly pressed, slice the strips into small cubes.

2. Bring the water and quinoa to a boil in a large pot over high heat. Once the water begins to boil, lower the heat, and simmer for about 15 minutes, or until the quinoa is tender, and the water has reduced. Transfer the pot to a wooden chopping board to cool.

3. In a medium-sized bowl, whisk together the honey, mustard, salt, pepper, vinegar, and olive oil.

4. Divide the baby arugula between 4 serving bowls, and top with equal amounts of the cooked quinoa. Garnish the quinoa with the chopped apple, and drizzle with the dressing.

5. Serve immediately.

Quick Tip:
Any leftovers can be refrigerated in an airtight container for no more than 5 days.

CHEESY VEGETARIAN PIZZA

COOK TIME: 25 MINS | MAKES: 6 SERVINGS

INGREDIENTS:

Dough:
- 2 1\4 tsp. rapid rising yeast
- 3\4 tsp. brown sugar
- 1 1\4 cups warm water
- 1 1\2 cups tapioca flour
- 2 1\2 cups unbleached all-purpose flour
- 1 1\2 tsp. kosher salt
- 6 tbsp. extra-virgin olive oil (divided)

Toppings:
- 2 tbsp. extra-virgin avocado oil
- 2 tsp. crushed garlic
- 28 oz. canned marinara sauce
- 8 oz. button mushrooms, sliced
- 1 tsp. dried basil
- 1 tsp. dried oregano
- 16 0z. mozzarella cheese, shredded
- 2 cups arugula

DIRECTIONS:

1. Set the oven to preheat to 475°F, with the wire rack in the center of the oven.

2. In a medium-sized glass bowl, whisk together the yeast, sugar, and water. Allow the yeast to bloom for 5 minutes on the counter.

3. In a large mixing bowl, whisk together the tapioca flour, all-purpose flour, and salt. Add the yeast mixture, and half of the olive oil. Stir the ingredients until the dough just comes together.

4. Turn the dough out onto a clean, lightly floured surface, and knead for 5 minutes, or until the dough is smooth and elastic.

5. Spread the final 3 tablespoons of the oil over a large, rimmed baking sheet in an even layer. Place the dough on the sheet, and cover with a damp kitchen towel. Allow the dough to rise in a warm area for 1 hour.

6. When the dough has doubled in size, knead again for 5 minutes, and roll the dough out to fit the sheet pan. Use a fork to poke holes all over the dough. Place the dough back on the pan, and cover with plastic wrap. Allow the dough to rise again for 1 hour.

7. When the dough has risen a second time, use a basting brush to coat the base with the avocado oil. Spread the crushed garlic over the base in an even layer. Place the base in the oven for 5 minutes, until the garlic becomes fragrant.

8. After 5 minutes, remove the base from the oven, and spread the marinara sauce over the garlic in an even layer.

9. Arrange the mushrooms on the sauce, and sprinkle with the basil and oregano. Top the pizza with cheese, and bake in the oven for 13-16 minutes, or until the cheese has melted, and the base is crispy.

10. Slice, and serve the pizza hot, topped with arugula.

Quick Tip:
Leftover pizza can be frozen for up to 2 months, or refrigerated for no more than 5 days in an airtight container. Reheat the pizza in the oven for 10 minutes at 350°F.

SWISS CHARD & STRAWBERRY SALAD

COOK TIME: 20-25 MINS | MAKES: 6 SERVINGS

INGREDIENTS:

- White of 1 large free-range egg
- 1 tsp. kosher salt (divided)
- 1 tsp. ground cinnamon
- 1\4 tsp. ground nutmeg
- 1 tsp. pure vanilla essence
- 1/2 cup raw wild honey (divided)
- 3 cups whole pecans
- 1\2 small red onion, sliced
- 3 cups strawberries, sliced
- 10 cups Swiss Chard, chopped
- 1\2 tsp. ground mustard powder
- 2 tsp. paleo mayonnaise
- 1 tbsp. poppy seeds
- 1\4 cup champagne vinegar
- 1\2 cup extra-virgin olive oil

DIRECTIONS:

1. Cover a large, rimmed baking sheet with greaseproof paper, and set the oven to preheat to 300°F, with the wire rack in the center of the oven.

2. In a medium-sized bowl, whisk the egg white to form soft peaks. Whisk in 1\2 teaspoon of salt, the cinnamon, nutmeg, vanilla essence, and 1\4 cup of honey. Gently fold in the pecans.

3. Scrape the mixture onto the prepared baking sheet in an even layer, using an offset spatula to smooth it out. Bake the sheet in the oven for 20-25 minutes, stirring after 10-12 minutes to prevent burning. Once the coating is firm, and adheres to the nuts, remove the tray from the oven, and cool for 15 minutes on the counter, or until the coating hardens.

4. When the pecans have hardened, toss them in a large bowl, together with the red onions, strawberries, and Swiss chard.

5. In a medium-sized mixing bowl, whisk together the remaining salt, remaining honey, mustard powder, paleo mayonnaise, poppy seeds, champagne vinegar, and olive oil.

6. Drizzle the dressing over the salad, and serve straight away.

BAKED SPROUTS IN AIOLI SAUCE

COOK TIME: 30-35 MINS | MAKES: 6-8 SERVINGS

INGREDIENTS:

- 2 lbs. Brussels sprouts, trimmed, and halved lengthwise
- 2 tbsp. extra-virgin avocado oil
- 1 1\4 tsp. Himalayan salt (divided)
- 1 tsp. white pepper (divided)
- 1 tsp. garlic powder
- 2 tsp. freshly squeezed lemon juice
- 4 canned chipotles in adobo sauce
- 1 cup paleo mayonnaise

DIRECTIONS:

1. Cover a large, rimmed baking sheet with greaseproof paper, and set the oven to preheat to 400°F, with the wire rack in the center of the oven.

2. In a large bowl, toss the halved Brussels sprouts with the oil, 1 teaspoon of salt, 1\2 teaspoon of pepper, and the garlic powder.

3. Fan the seasoned sprouts out on the prepared baking sheet, and bake in the oven for 30-35 minutes, or until the sprouts are cooked all the way through, and the edges are beginning to crisp.

4. In a high-powered food processor, pulse the remaining salt, remaining pepper, lemon juice, chipotles, and mayonnaise on high, until you have a lump-free mixture.

5. Serve the cooked sprouts drizzled with the aioli sauce.

SWISS CHARD & BEAN QUESADILLAS

COOK TIME: 5-10 MINS | MAKES: 2 SERVINGS

INGREDIENTS:

- 2 tbsp. fresh salsa, chilled
- 2 tbsp. fresh coriander leaves, chopped
- 1\2 cup canned no-salt-added black turtle beans, drained and rinsed
- Olive oil cooking spray
- 4 corn wraps
- 1\2 cup fresh Swiss chard, chopped
- 6 tbsp. mozzarella cheese, grated

DIRECTIONS:

1. In a medium-sized bowl, use a fork to whisk and mash the salsa, coriander leaves, and turtle beans.

2. Preheat a large, cast-iron frying pan over medium heat.

3. Generously coat the bottom of the preheated pan with olive oil spray. Place one wrap in the pan, and top it with half of the beans and salsa, half of the chard, and half of the cheese. Cover the filling with a second wrap, and coat the top wrap with olive oil spray. Fry the wrap for 2 minutes before flipping. Fry the other side for an additional 1-2 minutes, or until all the cheese has melted, and the wraps are lightly toasted.

4. Repeat the process with the remaining ingredients, and more olive oil spray.

5. Serve the quesadillas hot.

FRESH MINT ARTICHOKE RISOTTO

COOK TIME: 40 MINS | MAKES: 5 SERVINGS

INGREDIENTS:

- 4 cups vegetable stock
- 4 tbsp. extra-virgin avocado oil (divided)
- 1 small shallot, diced
- 4 oz. sugar snap peas, trimmed and halved
- 14 oz. canned artichoke hearts, drained and quartered
- 1 1\2 cups Arborio rice
- 1\2 tsp. Himalayan salt
- 1\2 tsp. white pepper
- 1\4 cup fresh mint leaves, chopped
- 1\4 cup fresh chives, chopped
- 1\3 cup fresh flat-leaf parsley, chopped
- 1\2 lemon, juiced

DIRECTIONS:

1. Bring the stock to a gentle simmer in a large saucepan over medium heat. When the stock is heated through, transfer the pot to a wooden chopping board while you prepare the rest of the dish.

2. In a large frying pan over medium heat, heat 2 tablespoons of the oil. When the oil is nice and hot, fry the shallots, peas, and artichoke hearts while stirring, until the hearts soften, and the shallots become transparent, about 6-8 minutes. Scrape the vegetables into a small bowl, and tent to keep warm.

3. In the same pan over medium heat, add the rest of the avocado oil. When the oil is hot, fry the rice and salt, while stirring continuously for 2-3 minutes. Don't panic if the rice begins to snap, crackle, and pop, as this is normal. Add 1 cup of the warmed stock to the pan, and stir for 5-8 minutes, or until all of the liquid has been absorbed. Continue to add one cup of stock at a time, and cook the risotto until you have used all the stock, or the rice has reached the desired level of tenderness. If all the stock has been used up, and the rice is still not tender enough, add water to the process, and continue cooking, using 1\3 cup of warm water at a time.

4. Scrape the cooked rice into a large serving bowl, and stir in the pepper, mint leaves, chives, parsley, and lemon juice.

5. Serve the warm vegetables on a bed of mint risotto.

Quick tip:
Any leftovers can be refrigerated in an airtight container for no more than 4 days, or frozen for up to 3 months.

YAM & BEAN ENCHILADAS

COOK TIME: 25-30 MINS | MAKES: 4 SERVINGS

INGREDIENTS:

- 2 tbsp. extra-virgin olive oil
- 2 medium yams, peeled and cubed (1-inch cubes)
- 1 red bell pepper, seeded and diced
- 1 small shallot, chopped
- 1\4 tsp. white pepper
- 1\2 tsp. Himalayan salt
- 1\2 tsp. onion powder
- 1\2 tsp. garlic powder
- 1 tsp. ground cumin
- 2 tsp. crushed garlic
- 10 oz. canned n0-sugar-added red enchilada sauce (divided)
- 3 tbsp. fresh coriander leaves, chopped (extra for garnish)
- 15 oz. canned black turtle beans, drained and rinsed
- 8 corn wraps

Optional Toppings:
- Creamy jalapeño ranch dressing
- Chopped avocados
- Chopped tomatoes
- Chopped jalapeño

DIRECTIONS:

1. Coat a large casserole dish with baking spray, and set the oven to preheat at 350°F, with the wire rack in the center of the oven.

2. Heat the olive oil in a large frying pan over medium heat. When the oil is nice and hot, add the yams, and fry for 10-12 minutes, or until the yams soften, and the edges become nice and crispy. Stir in the bell peppers and shallots for 3 minutes, before adding the pepper, salt, onion powder, garlic powder, cumin, and crushed garlic. Allow the flavors to meld for 1 minute before stirring in 3 tablespoons of the enchilada sauce, 3 tablespoons of the coriander leaves, and the black turtle beans. Stir until all of the ingredients are heated through, and transfer the pan to a wooden chopping board.

3. Heat the wraps in the microwave for 15-20 seconds. Place the warmed wraps, open, on a clean surface, and spoon about 3-5 tablespoons of the enchilada sauce onto each, spreading the sauce out in an even layer. Divide the yams and beans between the wraps. Fold the wraps like burritos, and arrange them in the prepared casserole dish, with the folds facing down. Pour the remaining enchilada sauce over all the wraps.

4. Bake the dish in the oven for 15 minutes, or until the sauce is heated through, and simmering.

5. Serve the enchiladas garnished with the extra coriander leaves, and toppings of your choice.

CURRIED CAULIFLOWER FLORETS

COOK TIME: 20 MINS | MAKES: 4 SERVINGS

INGREDIENTS:

- 2 tbsp. extra-virgin avocado oil
- 1 medium shallot, diced
- 2 tsp. crushed garlic
- 1\4 cup red curry paste
- 1 tsp. kosher salt
- 1 tsp. ground coriander seeds
- 2 tsp. ground ginger
- 4 cups cauliflower florets
- 3 medium carrots, peeled, and thinly sliced
- 15 oz. canned chickpeas, drained and rinsed
- 3\4 cup vegetable stock
- 1 tbsp. freshly squeezed lime juice
- 2 tbsp. coconut aminos
- 2 cups packed Swiss chard
- 13.5 oz. canned full-fat coconut milk
- Basmati rice, cooked, for serving
- Fresh coriander leaves, chopped, for garnish
- Lightly toasted cashew nuts, for garnish

DIRECTIONS:

1. In a large frying pan over medium heat, heat the olive oil. When the oil is nice and hot, fry the shallots for 5-6 minutes, or until they become transparent, stirring occasionally to prevent burning. Stir in the garlic, and fry for 1-2 minutes, allowing the flavors to meld. Stir in the red curry paste, salt, ground coriander seeds, and ground ginger, cooking for 1-2 additional minutes.

2. Stir in the cauliflower florets and carrots, and cook for 4-5 minutes, or until the vegetables begin to soften. You don't want to over-cook them at this point. Stir in the chickpeas and vegetable stock with the heat on high. When the stock begins to simmer, reduce the heat to low, and simmer for 8-10 minutes, until the cauliflower has completely softened.

3. Stir in the lime juice, coconut aminos, Swiss chard, and coconut milk for a few minutes, or until the chard leaves reduce in size.

4. Plate the curried cauliflower florets on a bed of cooked basmati rice, and garnish with the coriander leaves and cashews before serving.

SWEET SMOKED PAPRIKA BEAN BURGERS

COOK TIME: 30 MINS | MAKES: 6 SERVINGS

INGREDIENTS:

- 1 tbsp. extra-virgin olive oil
- 1 large shallot, diced
- 3 tsp. crushed garlic
- 1\2 red bell pepper, seeded and chopped
- 1\4 tsp. white pepper
- 1\2 tsp. kosher salt
- 1\2 tsp. chili powder
- 1 tsp. sweet smoked paprika
- 2 tsp. ground cumin
- 2 tbsp. paleo mayonnaise
- 2 tbsp. coconut aminos
- 3 tbsp. tapioca flour
- 15 oz. canned black turtle beans, rinsed and drained

DIRECTIONS:

1. Cover a large, rimmed baking pan with greaseproof paper, and set the oven to preheat to 375°F, with the wire rack in the center of the oven.

2. Heat the olive oil in a medium-sized pot over medium heat. When the oil is nice and hot, fry the shallots for 12-15 minutes, while stirring, or until the shallots are translucent, and slightly crispy. Scrape half of the shallots into a small bowl, and keep warm.

3. Add the garlic and bell peppers to the pot, and fry for about 2-3 minutes, or until the peppers begin to soften.

4. Scrape the cooked vegetables into a high-powered blender, along with the pepper, salt, chili powder, paprika, cumin, mayonnaise, coconut aminos, and tapioca flour. Pulse on high until everything is properly incorporated. Add 3\4 of the beans, and pulse again. Switch off the blender, and stir in the remaining beans.

5. Form the mixture into patties, using about 1\3 cup of the mixture per patty. Arrange the prepared patties on the prepared baking pan, and bake in the oven for about 12 minutes, flipping halfway through the cooking time, or until the patties are nicely browned.

6. Garnish the patties with the other half of the fried onions, and serve.

AVO-TOPPED VEGGIE WRAPS

COOK TIME: 10 MINS | MAKES: 4 SERVINGS

INGREDIENTS:

- 1 tbsp. extra-virgin avocado oil
- 1 zucchini, diced
- 1 small shallot, diced
- 15.5 oz. canned pinto beans, drained and rinsed
- 1\2 tsp. ground cumin
- 1\2 tsp. white pepper
- 1\2 tsp. kosher salt
- 1 small cabbage, grated
- 1 large avocado, diced
- 4 large corn wraps
- 1\2 cup fresh coriander leaves, chopped

DIRECTIONS:

1. Heat the oil in a large frying pan over medium heat. When the oil is nice and hot, fry the zucchini and shallots for 5-7 minutes, or until the vegetables soften. Stir occasionally to prevent burning. Stir in the beans, cumin, pepper, and salt for 1-2 minutes, or until the beans are heated through.

2. In a medium-sized bowl, stir together the cabbage and diced avocado.

3. Lay the wraps out on a clean surface. Divide the bean mixture between the wraps, and top with cabbage and avo. Garnish the wraps with the fresh coriander leaves before serving.

Quick Tip:
Any leftover wraps can be refrigerated in an airtight container for no more than 2 days. The wraps can also be frozen in tin foil for up to 2 months. Reheat the frozen wraps in the oven for 10-15 minutes at 350°F.

SOUPS & STEWS

MOROCCAN SPICED LENTIL STEW

COOK TIME: 25-30 MINS | MAKES: 6 SERVINGS

INGREDIENTS:

- 2 lbs. russet potatoes, peeled and quartered
- 3 tbsp. extra-virgin avocado oil
- 2 celery stalks, diced
- 1 small shallot, diced
- 3 medium carrots, peeled and diced
- 4 tsp. crushed garlic
- 1\2 tsp. white pepper (divided)
- 2 tsp. kosher salt (divided)
- 3\4 tsp. ground cinnamon
- 1 tsp. ground turmeric
- 1 1\2 tsp. ground cumin

- 2 tbsp. sweet smoked paprika
- 4 cups vegetable stock
- 1 1\4 cups red lentils
- 1 cup spinach
- 2 tbsp. freshly squeezed lemon juice
- 1\2 cup coconut cream
- 2 tbsp. ghee
- 1 tsp. baking powder
- 3-5 tbsp. almond milk
- Fresh coriander leaves, chopped, for garnish

DIRECTIONS:

1. Place the potatoes in a large pot of water, and boil over high heat until the potatoes have softened, about 15-18 minutes.

2. While the potatoes are boiling, heat the avocado oil in a large pot. When the oil is nice and hot, fry the celery, shallots, and carrots for 5 minutes, or until the shallots are translucent, and the carrots are beginning to soften. Stir in the garlic for 1 minute, allowing the flavors to meld. Stir in half of the pepper, half of the salt, and the cinnamon, turmeric, cumin, and paprika, until all of the spices are properly incorporated.

3. Pour the stock into the pot, and deglaze the bottom by scraping up any bits of food that have stuck to the bottom of the pot while you stir. Add the lentils, and stir. When the stock begins to boil, reduce the heat to medium-low, and simmer with the lid on the pot for 10-12 minutes, or until the lentils soften. Add the spinach and lemon juice, stirring for 2-3 minutes until the spinach has reduced in size.

4. When the potatoes are cooked, strain the water over the sink, and place the potatoes in a large mixing bowl. Mash with a fork, and stir in the coconut cream, ghee, and remaining salt and pepper. Beat in the baking powder, before adding the almond milk, 1 tablespoon at a time, until you have the desired consistency for the mash.

5. Serve the stew over a bed of mashed potatoes, and garnish with the fresh coriander leaves.

MEXICAN SPICED CHICKEN SOUP

COOK TIME: 6-8 HOURS | MAKES: 6 SERVINGS

INGREDIENTS:

- 1 tsp. kosher salt
- 1\2 tsp. white pepper
- 2 tsp. sweet smoked paprika
- 2 tsp. ground cumin
- 1 tbsp. chili powder
- 1\4 cup fresh coriander leaves, chopped (extra for garnish)
- 2 cups chicken stock
- 1 tbsp. freshly squeezed lime juice (extra for serving)
- 2 tsp. crushed garlic
- 2 bell peppers, chopped
- 1 1\2 cups frozen corn
- 14.5 oz. fire-roasted tomatoes
- 15 oz. canned black turtle beans, drained and rinsed
- 1 1\2 lbs. boneless chicken breasts, skins removed
- Avocado, diced, for serving

DIRECTIONS:

1. In a large slow cooker, stir together the salt, pepper, paprika, cumin, chili powder, coriander leaves, stock, lime juice, garlic, peppers, corn, tomatoes, and black beans. When all of the ingredients are properly combined, stir in the chicken breasts. Place the lid on the cooker, and cook on low for 6-8 hours, until the chicken is properly cooked.

2. When the chicken is properly cooked, shred the meat using a sharp knife.

3. Serve the soup topped with sliced avocado and coriander leaves, with a few extra squirts of lime juice.

BELL PEPPER RICE SOUP

COOK TIME: 5-6 HOURS | MAKES: 8 SERVINGS

INGREDIENTS:

- 1 1\2 tbsp. extra-virgin avocado oil
- 1 small shallot, diced
- 3 tsp. crushed garlic
- 4 cups beef stock
- 1 lb. ground beef
- 1\4 tsp. white pepper
- 1 tsp. kosher salt
- 1 tsp. dried dill
- 1 tsp. dried oregano
- 1 tsp. sweet smoked paprika
- 2 cups long-grain brown rice
- 14.5 oz. canned diced tomatoes, with the juices
- 14.4 oz. canned tomato sauce
- 1 green bell pepper, seeded and diced

DIRECTIONS:

1. In a large frying pan over medium-high heat, heat the avocado oil. When the oil is nice and hot, fry the shallots for 3-4 minutes, or until they become translucent. Stir in the garlic for 1-2 minutes, allowing the flavors to meld. Pour in the stock, and add the beef, stirring for 3-5 minutes, until the beef is properly cooked.

2. Scrape the beef into a large slow cooker, and stir in the pepper, salt, dill, oregano, paprika, rice, diced tomatoes, tomato sauce, and bell peppers.

3. Place a lid on the cooker, and cook on low for 5-6 hours.

4. Ladle the soup into bowls, and serve hot.

TURTLE BEAN & CORIANDER SOUP

COOK TIME: 15-20 MINS | MAKES: 4 SERVINGS

INGREDIENTS:

- 1 tbsp. avocado oil
- 1 cup shallots, finely chopped
- 1 tsp. ground cumin
- 2 tsp. crushed garlic
- 1\2 tsp. kosher salt
- 1\2 tsp. white pepper
- 3 cups no-salt-added vegetable stock
- 3\4 cup chilled fresh salsa
- 15 oz. canned no-salt-added black turtle beans, drained and rinsed
- 1 tbsp. freshly squeezed lime juice
- 2 tbsp. fresh coriander leaves, chopped
- 1\2 cup canned pumpkin puree

DIRECTIONS:

1. In a large pot over medium heat, heat the avocado oil. When the oil is nice and hot, fry the shallots for 4-5 minutes, or until they soften, and become translucent. Stir in the cumin and garlic, allowing the flavors to meld for 1 minute. Stir in the salt, pepper, stock, salsa, and beans. When the stock begins to boil, lower the heat to maintain a gentle simmer for 10 minutes, or until the soup begins to thicken. Stir the pot occasionally to prevent burning.

2. Stir in the lime juice, coriander leaves, and pureed pumpkin. Scoop half of the soup into a high-powered blender, and pulse on high until you have a lump-free mixture. You may want to cover the top of the blender, to prevent splattering and burning from the steam.

3. Scrape the smooth soup back into the pot, and stir to combine. When the soup is properly heated through, ladle into bowls, and serve.

ASIAN-STYLE NOODLE SOUP

COOK TIME: 20 MINS | MAKES: 4 SERVINGS

INGREDIENTS:

- 2 large free-range eggs, chilled
- 1 tbsp. extra-virgin olive oil
- 3 tbsp. red curry paste
- 2 tsp. fresh ginger, grated
- 3 tsp. crushed garlic
- 2 baby bok choy, whites and greens separated
- 2 medium carrots, thinly sliced
- 1 bell pepper, seeded and diced
- 4 cups vegetable stock
- 1 tsp. kosher salt
- 2 tsp. raw wild honey
- 1 tbsp. coconut aminos
- 13.5 oz. canned full-fat coconut milk
- 4 oz. packaged vermicelli noodles
- 1 lime, juiced
- 1\4 cup fresh coriander leaves, chopped
- 1\2 medium red onion, thinly sliced

DIRECTIONS:

1. Bring 1-inch of filtered water to a boil in a small pot over high heat. When the water begins to boil, add the chilled eggs, and boil uncovered for 6 minutes. Fill a medium-sized bowl with ice and cold water. After 6 minutes, transfer the boiled eggs to the ice bath, and set aside to cool.

2. Heat the olive oil in a large frying pan over medium heat. When the oil is nice and hot, fry the curry paste, ginger, and garlic for 1-2 minutes, until fragrant. Stir in the white parts of the bok choy stems, and the carrots, and bell peppers. When the vegetables are properly incorporated, pour in the stock. Raise the heat to medium-high, and bring the stock to a boil. Once the stock is boiling, lower the heat to medium-low, and maintain a gentle simmer for 4 minutes, until the carrots are soft.

3. Stir in the salt, honey, coconut aminos, and coconut milk. Add the green parts of the bok choy, and cook for 1-2 minutes, or until the leaves reduce in size.

4. Stir in the noodles, and simmer for 3 minutes while stirring, or until the noodles are properly cooked.

5. Peel the chilled eggs, and slice each in half.

6. Serve the noodles garnished with lime juice, coriander leaves, red onions, and sliced egg.

THAI-SPICED CHICKEN SOUP

COOK TIME: 5-10 MINUTES | MAKES: 4 SERVINGS

INGREDIENTS:

- 1 tbsp. extra-virgin avocado oil
- 2 tsp. crushed garlic
- 1 1\2 tbsp. fresh ginger, grated
- 2 tbsp. green curry paste
- 1\4 cup fresh coriander stems
- 13.5 oz. canned light coconut milk
- 1 tbsp. freshly squeezed lime juice (extra for serving)
- 1\2 cup filtered water
- 3 cups no-salt-added chicken stock
- 2 cups cooked rotisserie chicken, shredded
- 3 oz. raw brown rice vermicelli noodles
- Fresh coriander leaves for garnish

DIRECTIONS:

1. In a large, cast-iron pot over medium heat, heat the avocado oil. When the oil is nice and hot, fry the garlic and ginger for 1-2 minutes. Stir in the curry paste for 1 additional minute. Stir in the coriander stems, coconut milk, lime juice, water, and stock. Simmer the sauce for 10 minutes while stirring.

2. Add the shredded chicken and noodles, simmering for 3 minutes, or until the noodles reach the desired level of doneness.

3. Ladle the soup into bowls, and serve with the fresh coriander leaves, and the optional extra lime juice.

DELICIOUS CHARD & TOMATO SOUP

COOK TIME: 20 MINS | MAKES: 6 SERVINGS

INGREDIENTS:

- 1 tbsp. extra-virgin avocado oil
- 1 shallot, finely chopped
- 3\4 tsp. Himalayan salt (divided)
- 6 cups no-salt-added vegetable stock
- 1 fresh rosemary sprig
- 15 oz. canned no-salt-added navy beans, drained and rinsed
- 1 tbsp. tomato paste
- 26.5 oz. packaged tomatoes
- 3 tsp. crushed garlic
- 1\2 cup filtered water
- 1\2 cup whole raw cashews
- 2 tbsp. balsamic vinegar
- 1\3 cup fresh basil leaves, chopped
- 2 cups fresh Swiss chard

DIRECTIONS:

1. In a large pot over medium heat, heat the avocado oil. When the oil is nice and hot, fry the shallots for 4 minutes, or until tender. Stir in 1\2 teaspoon of salt, and the vegetable stock, rosemary, beans, tomato paste, tomatoes, and garlic. When the soup begins to boil, lower the heat, and simmer for 15 minutes, stirring at regular intervals to prevent burning.

2. Stir together the water and cashews in a microwave-safe dish. Heat the cashews in the microwave on high for 3 minutes. Discard the water. Stir the heated cashews into the pot.

3. Discard the fresh herbs before using an immersion blender to puree the soup. Add the remaining salt, along with the vinegar, basil, and chard, stirring to combine. Cook the soup for 2 minutes while stirring, or until the chard has reduced in size.

4. Ladle the soup into bowls, and serve hot.

ROASTED WINTER SQUASH SOUP

COOK TIME: 35 MINS | MAKES: 4 SERVINGS

INGREDIENTS:

- 4 garlic cloves, minced
- 1 small shallot, chopped
- 1 medium winter squash, peeled, seeded, and diced
- 1\4 cup sunflower oil
- Kosher salt
- 3 cups chicken bone stock
- 1 tsp. ground cinnamon
- 1 cup full-fat unsweetened coconut milk

DIRECTIONS:

1. Cover a large, rimmed baking pan with greaseproof paper, and set the oven to preheat to 400°F, with the wire rack in the center of the oven.

2. In a large bowl, toss together the garlic, shallots, squash, and sunflower oil. Season the bowl with salt to taste. Fan the vegetables out on the prepared baking pan, and bake in the oven for 25-30 minutes, or until the squash is fork-tender.

3. Meanwhile, bring the stock to a rolling boil over medium heat in a large pot. When the stock begins to boil, reduce the heat to maintain a gentle simmer. When the squash is tender, scrape the contents of the pan into the stock, and stir for 5 minutes.

4. Use a hand-held immersion blender to puree the soup in the pot.

5. Stir in the cinnamon and coconut milk. Taste the soup, and add more salted if needed.

6. If the soup is too thick, you may add additional bone stock, until the soup reaches the desired consistency.

7. Ladle the soup into bowls, and serve warm.

Quick Tip:
Any leftover soup can be refrigerated in an airtight container for no more than 4 days, or frozen for 3 months.

CARAMELIZED ONION SOUP

COOK TIME: 40 MINS | MAKES: 4 SERVINGS

INGREDIENTS:

- 1\4 cup extra-virgin avocado oil
- 2 white onions, thinly sliced
- 2 yellow onions, thinly sliced
- 1 tsp. coconut sugar
- 2 fresh thyme sprigs
- 2 whole bay leaves
- 2 tbsp. arrowroot starch
- 6 cups beef bone stock
- Kosher salt
- White pepper

DIRECTIONS:

1. In a large, cast-iron pot, heat the avocado oil over medium heat. Add the onions, coconut sugar, thyme, and bay leaves, frying for 4 minutes, until the onions become translucent. Place a lid on the pot, and allow the onions to caramelize for 20 minutes, stirring at regular intervals to prevent burning.

2. Drizzle the arrowroot starch over the caramelized onions, and gently whisk in the beef bone stock. Place the lid back on the pot, and simmer for an additional 20 minutes, stirring at regular intervals.

3. Discard the fresh herbs, and season the soup to taste with salt and pepper.

Quick Tip:
Any leftovers can be refrigerated in an airtight container for no more than 4 days.

THAI-INSPIRED SHRIMP SOUP

COOK TIME: 45 MINS | MAKES: 4 SERVINGS

INGREDIENTS:

- 1-inch fresh ginger, peeled
- 1 fresh lemongrass stalk, outer layers discarded
- 2 tbsp. freshly squeezed lime juice
- 1 lime, zested
- 4 cups chicken bone stock
- 1 cup button mushrooms, sliced
- 2 tbsp. fresh coriander leaves, chopped
- 1 tsp. pure maple syrup
- 1 tbsp. fish sauce
- 1 cup full-fat unsweetened coconut milk
- 1 lb. shrimp, peeled and deveined

DIRECTIONS:

1. Lightly smash the ginger and lemongrass with the back of a knife to release the flavors. Chop the lemongrass into 4-inch pieces.

2. In a large pot over medium heat, bring the ginger, lemongrass, lime juice, lime zest, and chicken stock to a boil. Once the broth is boiling, lower the heat, and simmer for 10 minutes, stirring occasionally to prevent burning. After 10 minutes, discard the ginger and lemongrass, along with any bits floating on the surface.

3. Stir in the mushrooms, and simmer for 25 minutes. Add the coriander leaves, syrup, fish sauce, coconut milk, and shrimp, frying for 4-5 minutes, or until the shrimp blush. Do not overcook the shrimp.

4. Ladle the soup into bowls, and serve immediately.

Quick Tip:
Any leftovers can be refrigerated in an airtight container for no more than 4 days.

SIMPLE ONION & MUSHROOM SOUP

COOK TIME: 30 MINS | MAKES: 4 SERVINGS

INGREDIENTS:

- 2 tbsp. extra-virgin olive oil
- 4 tsp. crushed garlic
- 1 shallot, thinly sliced
- 4 cups button mushrooms, sliced
- Pinch kosher salt
- 1 whole bay leaf
- 3 fresh thyme sprigs
- 6 cups beef bone stock
- 1 cup full-fat unsweetened coconut milk

DIRECTIONS:

1. Heat the olive oil in a large pot over medium heat. When the oil is nice and hot, fry the garlic, shallots, and mushrooms for 10 minutes, until the shallots become translucent, and the mushrooms darken in color. Stir in a large pinch of salt, along with the bay leaf, thyme, and beef bone stock. Lower the heat to maintain a gentle simmer. Place a lid on the pot, and cook for 20 minutes, stirring at regular intervals to prevent burning.

2. Discard the herbs before stirring in the coconut milk.

3. Use a hand-held immersion blender to puree the soup in the pot.

4. Ladle the hot soup into bowls, and serve.

Quick Tip:
Any leftovers can be refrigerated in an airtight container for no more than 4 days.

HEARTY CURRIED CHICKPEA STEW

COOK TIME: 45 MINS | MAKES: 5 SERVINGS

INGREDIENTS:

- 2 tbsp. extra-virgin avocado oil
- 1 medium shallot, diced
- 1-inch fresh ginger, grated
- 2 tsp. crushed garlic
- 1\2 tsp. kosher salt
- 1 tsp. white pepper
- 1 tsp. ground turmeric
- 15.5 oz. canned chickpeas, drained and rinsed
- 2 cups vegetable stock
- 15 oz. canned full-fat coconut milk
- 1 bunch Swiss chard

DIRECTIONS:

1. Heat the avocado oil in a large, cast-iron pot over medium heat. When the oil is nice and hot, fry the shallots for 4 minutes, or until they become translucent.

2. Stir in the ginger and garlic, allowing the flavors to meld for 2-4 minutes. You may deglaze the pot by adding 1 teaspoon of water at a time, and scraping the food off the bottom with a wooden spoon, if the food is sticking too much.

3. Stir in the salt, pepper, turmeric, and chickpeas for 5-7 minutes, or until the chickpeas get a crispy golden coating.

4. Stir in the stock and coconut milk. Once the stew begins to boil, lower the heat to maintain a gentle simmer for 30-35 minutes, or until the stew thickens. Stir at regular intervals to prevent burning.

5. Stir in the chard for 3-6 minutes, until the leaves reduce in size.

6. Let the stew stand for a few minutes before serving.

Quick Tip:
Any leftovers can be refrigerated in an airtight container for no more than 5 days, or frozen for up to 3 months. To reheat, let the stew thaw overnight, and microwave for 2-3 minutes on high.

ITALIAN SPINACH SOUP

COOK TIME: 30 MINS | MAKES: 4 SERVINGS

INGREDIENTS:

- 2 tbsp. extra-virgin olive oil
- 1 shallot, finely chopped
- 2 tsp. dried oregano
- 1 tsp. kosher salt
- 4 tsp. crushed garlic
- 3 carrots, thinly sliced
- 3 celery stalks, finely chopped
- 1 1\2 lbs. ground pork
- 6 cups chicken bone stock
- 1 cup coarsely chopped spinach

DIRECTIONS:

1. In a large pot over medium-high heat, heat the olive oil. When the oil is nice and hot, stir in the shallots, oregano, salt, garlic, carrots, and celery for 5 minutes, or until the vegetables become tender.

2. Stir in the ground pork, and cook for 5-8 minutes, or until the meat is nicely browned.

3. Pour the stock into the pot, and stir to combine. When the stock begins to boil, lower the heat to maintain a gentle simmer for 20 minutes. After 20 minutes, add the spinach, and simmer for a few more minutes, until the leaves wilt. Season to taste with extra salt if needed.

4. Serve the soup hot.

Quick Tip:
Any leftovers can be stored in the fridge in an airtight container for no more than 4 days, or frozen for 3 months.

VIETNAMESE BEEF SOUP

COOK TIME: 20 MINS | MAKES: 6 SERVINGS

INGREDIENTS:

- 4 tsp. crushed garlic
- 1 whole cinnamon stick
- 6-inches of fresh ginger, peeled, and halved lengthwise
- 7 oz. packaged shirataki noodles
- 10 cups beef bone stock
- 1\4 cup fish sauce
- 2 tsp. pure maple syrup
- 1 tsp. kosher salt
- 1\4 cup whole Thai basil leaves
- 1\4 cup coriander leaves, chopped
- 2 spring onions, finely chopped
- 1 lb. raw flank steak, finely sliced against the grain
- 1 lime, sliced into 6 wedges

DIRECTIONS:

1. Stir together the garlic, cinnamon, ginger, noodles, stock, fish sauce, syrup, and salt in a large pot over medium heat. When the stock begins to boil, reduce the heat to maintain a gentle simmer, and cook covered for 20 minutes, stirring at regular intervals.

2. Discard the ginger, cinnamon, and any small bits floating on the surface.

3. Divide the basil leaves, coriander leaves, spring onions, steak, and noodles between 6 serving bowls. Spoon the hot soup over everything in the bowls; the steak will cook in the soup.

4. Serve the bowls hot, with the lime wedges on the side.

Quick Tip:
Any leftovers can be refrigerated in an airtight container for no more than 4 days.

BEEFY VEGETABLE STEW

COOK TIME: 35 MINS | MAKES: 4 SERVINGS

INGREDIENTS:

- 4 tbsp. extra-virgin olive oil (divided)
- Kosher salt
- 1 1\2 lbs. beef stew meat, patted dry
- 1\4 cup carrots, finely chopped
- 1 shallot, finely chopped
- 1\2 cup celery, finely chopped
- 1 cup porcini mushrooms, sliced
- 4 tsp. crushed garlic
- 1 tsp. dried thyme
- 1 tsp. dried oregano
- 1 tbsp. fresh parsley, finely chopped
- 6 cups beef bone stock

DIRECTIONS:

1. In a large bowl, use clean hands to massage a large pinch of salt into the meat.

2. Heat 2 tablespoons of the oil in a large pot over medium heat. When the oil is nice and hot, fry the seasoned meat for about 4 minutes, until nicely browned. Fry the meat in batches if all of it does not comfortably fit into the pot. Scrape the cooked meat into a bowl, and set aside.

3. Heat the remaining 2 tablespoons of oil in the same pot over medium heat. When the oil is nice and hot, fry the carrots, shallots, celery, and mushrooms for 4 minutes, until the mushrooms darken in color. Stir in the crushed garlic for 1 additional minute, allowing the flavors to meld.

4. Scrape the cooked beef back into the pot, along with the thyme, oregano, parsley, and beef bone stock. When the stock begins to boil, lower the heat to maintain a gentle simmer for 20 minutes, with the lid on the pot. Stir the stew at regular intervals to prevent burning.

5. Serve immediately.

Quick Tip:
Any leftovers can be stored in the fridge in an airtight container for no more than 4 days, or frozen for up to 3 months.

GINGERY CARROT & TURMERIC SOUP

COOK TIME: 40 MINS | MAKES: 5 SERVINGS

INGREDIENTS:

- 2 tbsp. extra-virgin avocado oil
- 1 small shallot, diced
- 1 cup winter squash, cubed
- 4 medium carrots, chopped
- 1 tbsp. ground turmeric
- 1-inch fresh ginger, grated
- 1 tsp. Himalayan salt
- 1 tsp. white pepper
- 13.5 oz. canned lite coconut milk
- 3 cups vegetable stock
- 1\3 cup fresh parsley leaves, chopped

DIRECTIONS:

1. Heat the oil in a large pot over medium heat. When the oil is nice and hot, fry the shallots, squash, and carrots until the vegetables are tender, and the shallots become transparent.

2. Stir in the turmeric, ginger, salt, and pepper for 2 minutes, allowing the flavors to meld. Pour in the coconut milk and stock, stirring to combine. When the soup begins to boil, reduce the heat to maintain a gentle simmer, and cook covered for 20 minutes. Stir the pot at regular intervals to prevent burning.

3. When all of the vegetables are fork-tender, use a hand-held immersion blender to puree the soup in the pot.

4. Ladle the hot soup into bowls, and serve garnished with the parsley leaves.

Quick Tip:
Any leftovers can be refrigerated in an airtight container for no more than 4 days, or frozen for up to 3 months.

SNACKS & SIDES

LEMON GRILLED OYSTERS

COOK TIME: 10 MINS | MAKES: 4 SERVINGS

INGREDIENTS:

- 24 fresh oysters in their shells
- Flaky sea salt
- White pepper
- 1\2 lime, juiced

DIRECTIONS:

1. Set the grill to preheat on high.

2. With the flattest side against the grill, cook the oysters for 5-10 minutes, or until they open.

3. Crack off the top half of each oyster shell, leaving the oysters in the bottom half.

4. Transfer the grilled oysters to a serving platter. Season the oysters to taste with salt and pepper. Drizzle the lime juice evenly over the oysters, and serve straight away.

Quick Tip:
Discard any oysters that have opened before cooking, as this means they are not safe to eat.

CORIANDER & LIME TURTLE BEANS

COOK TIME: 10 MINS | MAKES: 5 SERVINGS

INGREDIENTS:

- 1 tbsp. extra-virgin olive oil
- 1 whole garlic clove, crushed
- 15.5 oz. canned black turtle beans, drained and rinsed
- 1\2 tsp. kosher salt
- 1\3 tsp. white pepper
- 1 tsp. ground cumin
- 1 lime, juiced

DIRECTIONS:

1. Heat the olive oil in a small pot over medium heat. When the oil is nice and hot, fry the garlic for 1-3 minutes, or until fragrant and nicely toasted.

2. Stir in the beans, salt, pepper, cumin, and lime juice. Cook the beans for 4-6 minutes until heated through, stirring at regular intervals. If you would like varying textures in the dish, use a fork to mash some of the beans into the sauce.

3. Allow the beans to cool slightly before serving.

Quick Tip:
Any leftovers can be refrigerated in an airtight container for no more than 5 days.

GREEK-STYLE FLATBREAD

COOK TIME: 15-20 MINS | MAKES: 4 SERVINGS

INGREDIENTS:

- 1\2 tsp. Himalayan salt (plus 1\8 tsp.)
- 1\2 tsp. baking soda
- 1\4 cup grated parmesan cheese
- 1 1\2 cups blanched almond flour
- 1 large free-range egg, lightly beaten
- 2 tbsp. almond milk
- 2 tsp. extra-virgin olive oil
- 2 heirloom tomatoes, thinly sliced
- 4 oz. mozzarella cheese, grated
- 1\3 cup fresh basil leaves, torn
- Store-bought balsamic glaze

DIRECTIONS:

1. In a medium-sized mixing bowl, whisk together 1\2 teaspoon of salt, and the baking soda, parmesan cheese, and almond flour. Beat in the egg and milk, until all of the ingredients come together. Using clean hands, bring the dough together, and knead for 5 minutes until the dough is smooth. Divide the dough in half, and cover with plastic wrap. Chill the dough for 30 minutes, or until it is firm to the touch.

2. Set the oven to preheat to 350°F, with the wire rack in the center of the oven. Coat a large, rimmed baking pan with cooking spray.

3. Once the dough is chilled, and firm to the touch, roll each piece into an oblong shape of about 1\4-inch thick, using greaseproof paper above and below the dough as you roll it, to prevent sticking. Place the dough side by side on the prepared baking pan, and bake in the oven for about 13 minutes, or until the edges of the dough begin to crisp.

4. Remove the pan from the oven, and use a basting brush to coat the bread with 1 teaspoon of oil on each. Arrange the sliced tomatoes on the bread in an even layer, and sprinkle the mozzarella on top, leaving about an inch of bread open right around the edge to create a border.

5. Return the tray to the oven for 4-6minutes, allowing the cheese to melt. Season the hot bread with the remaining salt. Garnish with fresh basil leaves and balsamic glaze before serving.

6. Serve hot.

CHOCOLATEY PEANUT BUTTER BITES

COOK TIME: 0 MINS | MAKES: 24 SERVINGS

INGREDIENTS:

- 3\4 tsp. Himalayan salt
- 1 tbsp. pure vanilla essence
- 3 tbsp. coconut milk
- 6 tbsp. coconut sugar
- 1\2 cup natural peanut butter
- 15 oz. canned no-salt-added chickpeas, drained and rinsed
- 1 1\2 cups old-fashioned rolled oats
- 2\3 cup dark chocolate chips

DIRECTIONS:

1. In a high-powered blender, pulse the salt, vanilla, coconut milk, coconut sugar, peanut butter, and chickpeas on high, until you have a lump-free mixture. You may want to pause every now and then to scrape down the sides of the blender. The process should take about 1-2 minutes.

2. Gradually add 1 cup of oats to the blender, pulsing, and scraping the sides, until you, once again, have a lump-free batter. Scrape the mixture into a medium-sized bowl, and stir in the remaining oats, and the chocolate chips.

3. Roll the mixture into 24 balls of roughly the same size. Arrange the balls on a baking sheet, and chill, covered in cling wrap, for at least 1 hour.

4. Serve the peanut butter bites chilled.

Quick Tip:
The bites can also be frozen in an airtight container. Use greaseproof paper to separate the bites while freezing. To serve, allow the bites to defrost at room temperature for 10 minutes.

CORIANDER & LIME AVOCADO HUMMUS

COOK TIME: 0 MINS | MAKES: 4 SERVINGS

INGREDIENTS:

- 3 tbsp. filtered water
- 1\2 tsp. crushed red pepper (optional)
- 1\4 tsp. freshly ground black pepper
- 1\4 tsp. Himalayan salt
- 1\2 tsp. ground cumin
- 1 tsp. crushed garlic
- 3 tbsp. freshly squeezed lime juice
- 1\4 cup fresh coriander leaves, chopped
- 1 small ripe avocado, pitted and peeled
- 2 tbsp. extra-virgin olive oil
- 15 oz. canned no-salt-added chickpeas, drained and rinsed

DIRECTIONS:

1. Place all of the ingredients in a high-powered blender, and pulse on high until you have a smooth paste. You will need to pause now and then, to scrape down the sides of the blender. If the hummus is too thick, add more filtered water, 1 tablespoon at a time, until you have the desired consistency.

2. Scrape the hummus into a serving bowl, and chill, covered with cling wrap, until ready to serve.

OVEN-BAKED SPINACH CHIPS

COOK TIME: 15 MINS | MAKES: 4 SERVINGS

INGREDIENTS:

- 2 lbs. savoy spinach
- 1\2 tsp. kosher salt
- 3 tbsp. extra-virgin olive oil

DIRECTIONS:

1. Set the oven to preheat to 375°F, with the wire rack in the center of the oven, and line a large, rimmed baking tray with greaseproof paper.

2. Use a sharp knife to remove the spinach stems, and cut the larger leaves down to roughly the same size.

3. Use a large mixing bowl to toss the spinach leaves with the salt and olive oil, until all the leaves are evenly coated and seasoned.

4. Arrange the seasoned spinach on the prepared baking tray, and bake in the oven until the leaves are crispy, about 15 minutes.

5. Let the chips cool on the counter before serving.

HAM-WRAPPED CANTALOUPE SLICES

COOK TIME: 0 MINS | MAKES: 4 SERVINGS

INGREDIENTS:

- 1\2 ripened cantaloupe
- 5 slices hickory-smoked ham
- 1\2 tsp. crushed thyme
- 1 tsp. pure maple syrup

DIRECTIONS:

1. Place the cantaloupe on a wooden chopping board, and use a sharp knife to remove the rind. Cut the cantaloupe into 2 x 2-inch-thick strips.

2. Cut the ham into thin strips, and wrap each cantaloupe piece in a strip of ham.

3. Arrange the wrapped cantaloupe slices on a serving plate. Garnish the slices with thyme, and drizzle with syrup.

4. Serve, and enjoy.

Quick Tip:
Any leftovers can be refrigerated in an airtight container for no more than 4 days.

HONEY-DIPPED ROSEMARY PECANS

COOK TIME: 20 MINS | MAKES: 4-8 SERVINGS

INGREDIENTS:

- 1 tbsp. raw wild honey
- 1 tbsp. sunflower oil
- 1 tbsp. fresh rosemary leaves, finely chopped
- 2 cups unsalted pecan halves
- 1\8 tsp. cayenne pepper
- 3\4 tsp. Himalayan salt

DIRECTIONS:

1. Cover a large, rimmed baking sheet with tin foil. Coat the tin foil with a light layer of baking spray and set the oven to preheat to 325°F, with the wire rack in the center of the oven.

2. In a small glass bowl, combine the honey, sunflower oil, and rosemary leaves. Microwave on high for 10-second intervals, until the mixture reaches drizzling consistency.

3. In a medium-sized bowl, toss the pecan halves with the honey mixture, until all the nuts are evenly coated.

4. Fan the coated pecans out on the prepared baking sheet, and sprinkle the cayenne pepper and salt in an even layer.

5. Bake in the oven for 20 minutes, or until the coating hardens, and the nuts are nicely toasted.

6. Cool completely before serving.

Quick Tip:
Cooled nuts can be stored in the cupboard for no more than 1 week in an airtight container.

DESSERTS

NUTTY DARK CHOCOLATE BITES

COOK TIME: 0 MINS | MAKES: 12 SERVINGS

INGREDIENTS:

- 1\2 tsp. kosher salt (divided)
- 1 1\2 tsp. pure vanilla essence (divided)
- 2 tsp. raw wild honey
- 3 tbsp. pure cocoa powder
- 1\4 cup melted coconut oil, cooled slightly (plus 2 tbsp.)
- 1\2 cup creamy cashew butter (plus 1\3 cup)

DIRECTIONS:

1. Line a 12-slot muffin tin with cupcake liners.

2. In a medium-sized mixing bowl, whisk together half of the salt, 1 teaspoon vanilla, the honey, the cocoa powder, 1\4 cup coconut oil, and 1\2 cup of the cashew butter. When you have a smooth mixture, fill each cupcake liner with 1 tablespoon of the mixture. Set the rest aside at room temperature.

3. Place the muffin tin in the freezer for 10 minutes.

4. In a clean bowl, whisk together the remaining ingredients. Divide the mixture between the 12 frozen cupcake liners in an even layer. Top each liner with the remaining chocolate mixture, and use the back of a teaspoon to smooth out the top.

5. Freeze the bites for an additional 10 minutes before serving.

PUMPKIN SPICED SHEET CHEESE CAKE

COOK TIME: 0 MINS | MAKES: 16 SERVINGS

INGREDIENTS:

- 2 cups raw, unsalted cashews
- 2 cups lightly toasted pecans
- 1 1\4 cups pitted dates
- 1\4 tsp. kosher salt (plus 1\2 tsp.)
- 1 tbsp. filtered water
- 1\8 tsp. ground nutmeg
- 1\4 tsp. ground cloves
- 1\2 tsp. ground ginger
- 1 1\2 tsp. ground cinnamon
- 2 tsp. pure vanilla essence
- 1 tbsp. molasses
- 1\4 cup coconut oil, melted and slightly cooled
- 1\3 cup raw wild honey
- 1\3 cup canned pumpkin puree
- 1\2 cup canned coconut cream

DIRECTIONS:

1. In a large mixing bowl, cover the cashews in a few inches of filtered water. Seal the bowl with cling wrap, and chill overnight, or for 8-12 hours.

2. Cover a large, rimmed baking sheet with greaseproof paper.

3. In a blender, pulse the pecans, dates, and 1\4 teaspoon of salt for 1-2 minutes, until the ingredients come together to form a sticky dough. If the dough isn't quite coming together, add the filtered water, and pulse until it does. Scrape the dough out onto the prepared baking sheet in an even layer. Press the dough into the sheet, using your fingers or an offset spatula. The bottom of a clean glass will work even better.

4. Drain the cashews in a colander set over the sink.

5. In a clean blender, pulse the drained cashews, remaining salt, nutmeg, cloves, ginger, cinnamon, vanilla, molasses, coconut oil, honey, pumpkin puree, and coconut cream, until you have a smooth batter with no visible nut chunks. This should take 1-2 minutes in a high-powered blender.

6. Scrape the mixture onto the date crust on the baking sheet, and use an offset spatula to smooth out the surface. Gently tap the sheet on the counter to let out any trapped air. Place the sheet on a level surface in the freezer for 2 1\2 hours, or until the cheesecake is completely set.

7. Slice the cake into 16 blocks, and serve.

CHOCOLATE & HONEY CHIA PUDDING

COOK TIME: 0 MINS | MAKES: 5 SERVINGS

INGREDIENTS:

- 1\2 cup chia seeds
- 1 1\2 cups unsweetened almond milk
- 1 tsp. pure vanilla essence
- 2 tbsp. raw wild honey
- 2 tbsp. pure cocoa powder
- 1\3 tsp. kosher salt

DIRECTIONS:

1. Whisk the chia seeds, almond milk, vanilla essence, honey, cocoa powder, and salt together in a medium-sized bowl, until all of the ingredients are properly incorporated.

2. Seal the bowl with cling wrap, and chill for 30 minutes.

3. After 30 minutes, whisk the pudding again. Repeat this process every 30 minutes for 4 hours, until the pudding is nice and thick. This will prevent the pudding from setting in uneven layers.

4. Spoon the pudding into 5 serving bowls, and enjoy.

Quick Tip:
Leftover pudding can be refrigerated in an airtight container for no more than 5 days, or frozen for 2 months. To thaw the pudding, leave the frozen pudding in the fridge for a few hours. If it has become too thick, whisk in a few teaspoons of almond milk.

STRAWBERRY MAPLE POPS

COOK TIME: 0 MINS | MAKES: 10 SERVINGS

INGREDIENTS:

- 2 tbsp. fresh mint leaves, chopped
- 1 tbsp. freshly squeezed lemon juice
- 1\3 cup pure maple syrup
- 5 1\2 cups chopped strawberries
- 1 tsp. pure vanilla essence

DIRECTIONS:

1. In a food processor, pulse the mint leaves, lemon juice, maple syrup, strawberries, and vanilla on high, until all of the ingredients are properly combined, about 1-2 minutes.

2. Strain the mixture through a fine-mesh sieve, and discard all the leaves and seeds. Pour the mixture into pop molds, and freeze for 3 hours, or until the pops are solid. Serve, and enjoy.

Quick Tip:
Running the pop molds under warm water will make removing the pops much easier.

COCONUT HONEY COOKIES

COOK TIME: 10 MINS | MAKES: 12 SERVINGS

INGREDIENTS:

- 3 tbsp. coconut oil, melted
- 1 tbsp. coconut sugar
- 2 tbsp. raw wild honey
- 1 tsp. ground cinnamon
- 1\4 tsp. baking powder
- 1 tbsp. coconut flour
- 2 tbsp. cassava flour
- 1\2 cup tiger nut flour
- 1\2 cup shredded coconut
- 1\3 tsp. kosher salt
- 1 gelatin egg

DIRECTIONS:

1. Cover a large, rimmed baking pan with greaseproof paper, and set the oven to preheat to 375°F, with the wire rack in the center of the oven.

2. In a large bowl, whisk together the coconut oil, coconut sugar, honey, cinnamon, baking powder, coconut flour, cassava flour, tiger nut flour, shredded coconut, and salt. Beat in the gelatin egg, until all of the ingredients are properly incorporated.

3. Form the dough into 12 balls of roughly the same size. Arrange the balls on the prepared baking pan, and use the bottom of a clean glass to press the balls into cookies.

4. Place the pan in the oven for 8-10 minutes, or until the cookies are nicely browned.

5. Allow the cookies to cool on the pan for 10 minutes before serving.

Quick Tip:
Any leftover cookies can be refrigerated for no more than 1 week in an airtight container, or frozen for 3 months. To thaw, leave the cookies on the counter for 30 minutes before serving.

NUTTY HONEY BROWNIES

COOK TIME: 25-30 MINS | MAKES: 16 SERVINGS

INGREDIENTS:

- 1 tsp. pure vanilla essence
- Yolk of 1 large egg
- 2 whole large eggs
- 1\3 cup raw wild honey
- 1\2 cup coconut sugar
- 1 cup creamy almond butter
- 1\2 tsp. baking soda
- 1\2 tsp. kosher salt
- 1\3 tsp. ground nutmeg
- 2 tbsp. coconut flour
- 1\3 cup unsweetened cocoa powder
- 1\3 cup dairy-free chocolate chips

DIRECTIONS:

1. Cover a large, rimmed baking sheet with greaseproof paper, with some of the paper hanging over the edges to serve as handles. Set the oven to preheat to 350°F, with the wire rack in the center of the oven.

2. Whisk the vanilla, egg yolk, whole eggs, honey, coconut sugar, and almond butter together in a large bowl, until you have a smooth batter.

3. In a medium-sized bowl, whisk together the baking soda, salt, nutmeg, coconut flour, and cocoa powder. Gently beat the wet ingredients into the bowl of dry ingredients, and when all of the ingredients are properly combined in a thick dough, fold in the chocolate chips.

4. Scrape the batter out onto the prepared baking sheet, and spread the mixture out in an even layer. Bake in the oven for 25-30 minutes, or until an inserted skewer comes out almost clean, with a few crumbs still sticking to it.

5. Allow the brownies to cool on the pan for 10-15 minutes, before slicing them into 16 squares. Use the paper handles to lift the brownies out of the pan. Cool the brownies completely on a wire rack before serving.

BANANA MAPLE SOFT SERVE

COOK TIME: 0 MINS | MAKES: 1 SERVING

INGREDIENTS:

- 1 ripe banana, peeled and thinly sliced
- 1 tsp. pure maple syrup
- 1\3 tsp. ground cinnamon

DIRECTIONS:

1. Line a large, rimmed baking sheet with greaseproof paper.

2. Arrange the banana slices in a single layer on the prepared baking sheet. Freeze the bananas for a minimum of 2 hours.

3. In a high-powered food processor, pulse the frozen bananas, maple syrup, and cinnamon until you have a smooth paste.

4. Scrape the mixture into serving bowls. Enjoy immediately.

BUTTERY HONEY-DIPPED FRUIT

COOK TIME: 0 MINS | MAKES: 8 SERVINGS

INGREDIENTS:

- 3 tbsp. almond butter
- 1 cup plain Greek yogurt
- 1 tbsp. raw wild honey
- 1\3 tsp. ground cinnamon
- 2 cups fresh strawberries
- 2 firm bananas, halved in the middle

DIRECTIONS:

1. Cover a large, rimmed baking sheet with greaseproof paper.

2. In a large bowl, whisk together the butter, yogurt, honey, and cinnamon.

3. Dip the fruit in the mixture, and arrange them on the prepared baking sheet.

4. Enjoy as is, or cover the tray with cling wrap, and freeze for 20 minutes before serving, for a cold treat.

Made in United States
North Haven, CT
28 February 2022